My Autobiographies

MY AUTOBIOGRAPHIES

AN INTRODUCTION
TO PAST LIFE EXPLORATION
FOR PERSONAL AND SPIRITUAL
GROWTH

JOHN KOENIG

gatekeeper press
Columbus, Ohio

My Autobiographies: An Introduction to Past Life Exploration for Personal And Spiritual Growth

Published by **Gatekeeper Press**
2167 Stringtown Rd, Suite 109
Columbus, OH 43123-2989
www.GatekeeperPress.com

The cover design, interior formatting, typesetting, and editorial work for this book are entirely the product of the author. Gatekeeper Press did not participate in and is not responsible for any aspect of these elements.

ISBN (paperback): 9781662921513
eISBN: 9781662921520

For Maria
the love of my lives

TABLE OF CONTENTS

INTRODUCTION

Autobiographies? Plural?

Yes.

You see, this is *not* the autobiography of the person who is telling these stories. This little book is the autobiography of the Soul that resides within the body that writes these words. And its story is many, many autobiographies rolled into one.

It is also your story as this book is your invitation to undertake your own past life explorations – to see how lives you may have lived before may be shaping the circumstances, opportunities and challenges you face today.

I mention this because I doubt that the chronicle of my current incarnation would hold your attention for very long. I am <u>not</u> famous. I am not a captain of industry, a famous artist, or internationally renowned humanitarian. Nor am I infamous: I have never been caught committing some great crime that captured the world's attention.

And, likely – given the law of averages – you are more or less an ordinary person too. Unique. Special. But by the world's standards more or less invisible other than to your family, co-workers, neighbors and social acquaintances.

That is not to say that you, like me, have not had some successes and not committed some crimes. But, from the world's perspective, I am just an ordinary, somewhat elderly man living in the suburbs - married to the same woman approaching 50 years now with children and grandchildren. Professionally, I have enjoyed moderate success as an advertising writer. But the products I wrote commercials for are far more famous than I will ever be.

For the past 20 years or so, I have pursued a second career as a hypnotist. I have been privileged to help thousands of people quit smoking, lose weight, build careers, handle health issues, and overcome barriers to happiness and full self-expression.

Hopefully, there are more adventures, triumphs, and challenges yet to come for me. But I know my current incarnation is nearing its inevitable end. Not that I am complaining. It has been a good life as lives go. I am at peace with it and with myself. But my life story is not the stuff that would warrant an autobiography worth reading by anyone even at a low e-book price.

My Soul, on the other hand, has had quite a few interesting experiences. It is these that I will relate to you in the hope that *its* autobiographies may inspire you to think of your life from a different perspective. Perhaps you will even be inspired to engage in your own past life explorations.

So your invitation is to read this little book from the perspective of what your autobiographies might sound like and how you might integrate your past life experiences into your current incarnation.

The question of who I am will hopefully become unimportant as you read these pages. But you may find that the question of who you are will take on new depth. Remember the caterpillar in Lewis Carroll's *Alice in Wonderland*? When he asked Alice "who are you?", he was asking her to do more than recite her resume. He was asking Alice to describe her essence. Who was she from the broadest possible perspective? And I would suggest that the broadest perspective of my "life" or yours is that of a soul having a physical experience. These experiences usually occur one at a time, as far as we are aware. But the veil between our lives is thin, and with a little intention and guidance, it can be breached. We can then live from a higher point of view: that of a Soul observing and learning from its experiences incarnated as a human being. As you listen to my Soul's stories, I will be subtly asking you whether your spirit – your essence – has been here before and perhaps will be again in a different form. You will be asked to consider the possibility that your choices and mine are part of a broader plan: not simply for your individual soul's personal growth but also for the evolution of our species.

Who am I to write such a book? After all, I have admitted already to being an ordinary person. I see myself as a reflection of the roles I play in this life: husband, father, grandfather, mentor, coach, active member in the recovery community, spiritual seeker (and I am happy to say, spiritual finder), generally a positive force in my world and part of humanity's evolution. I am an ordinary person, yet one who is aware of being part of something much bigger.

Past-life exploration has been a major part of my journey. This book suggests the same is possible for you. All it takes is willingness, an open mind, and the investment of some time and energy – hopefully assisted by the right guide for you in your spiritual journey. You can consider this book your invitation to join me in this evolutionary journey. I should point out that you are not going to be reading here the exploits of someone who thinks he was Julius Caesar, Plato, Adolph Hitler, Shakespeare, Joan of Arc, or Jesus Christ for that matter. You need to know that even in my prior lives I was never especially famous or infamous either. Not a great king, well-known performer, artist of special note, or even world-class villain. My Soul (like most souls) seems to choose lives of obscurity. Humble people. Anonymous to the world stage. Everyday working men and women. Yet each of them had a beauty and importance that I feel called upon to share with you. And, I believe, each is as important and valuable as the life of any king, queen, emperor, or legendary historical figure. If this little work inspires you to journey into your own Soul's biographies, you will likely find the same. There is usually only one king or queen, a handful of nobles, and then the rest of us.

So, you know a little about me now. But how about you? Why should you spend your valuable time with me and my stories?

I am going to assume that you are curious about the idea of reincarnation or you would not have started this journey with me. You also know that, for over a billion Hindus and Buddhists, the idea that each soul leads life-after-life is a commonly accepted belief. Maybe you have read some books on the subject like *Many Lives Many Masters* by Brian Weiss, Raymond Moody's *Life After Life*, or Michael Newton's *Journey of Souls,* or Ian Stevenson's *Twenty Cases Suggestive of Reincarnation*. Perhaps you have seen reincarnation covered in

12

a documentary such a Netflix's *Surviving Death*. You might even have been to a past life therapist as part of your spiritual search. At the very least, you are curious. What if you have lived before? What if you will live again in a new body, maybe a different gender, race, circumstance? What will it be like for you to live your current life from that perspective?

Let me suggest you will find living as a Soul incarnated in a body it chose for personal development will add richness to your experience of life. I promise you it will give you a sense of that transformative day in the near or distant future: the day you die not as an end but merely as an important transition. My intention is that my explorations of past lives may be inspiring to you – that hearing the experiences that led me to choose my current life may help you better understand why you choose yours – including the people you chose as your teachers. Often these teachers appear in the unlikely form of parents, grandparents, brothers, sisters, children, business partners, neighbors: the people we love and who sometimes rub us the wrong way. I hope that you will discover that by re-experiencing these past lives, you will see how the learnings and challenges you faced in these "lives" can be integrated to help you make the most of your current life. And, in a broader sense, I will feel my job was well done if this little work inspires you to see your experience as part of something much broader. This broader context is the evolution of all humanity into something quite different, perhaps even a new species – one more closely allied with The Great Creator Itself.

You were probably not raised to think about life or your spiritual journey this way. You were most likely brought up to think of life as a single, continuous straight-line story: a linear narrative that began at your birth and continues until your death. After death? This was probably not something you thought about much in your early years. Like most of us, you were probably more consumed with living your life consumed by the here and now, not the hereafter. If death did cross your mind, the religion of your childhood suggested an afterlife. Here, you would be judged. You will either be rewarded by being sent to heaven for everlasting bliss or condemned to hell for endless torment. No do-overs allowed. No levels of heaven or degrees of hell. Just a simple and brutal PASS/FAIL system.

I found the religion of my childhood – Roman Catholicism – very satisfying when I was a child. I grew up imagining a loving Jesus Christ whose rather stern and distant Father was the real God: God the Father as we called Him. As I matured and began to come to terms with life issues, I came to believe that this God I was taught basically did not like me very much. In fact, I had the clear impression that God wanted me to go to hell for a life of torture. Why? Because that is what the nuns and brothers told us. A mortal sin would consign you automatically to an afterlife of everlasting torment. And it was as easy to incur a mortal sin as to act on an "impure thought." Of course, most adolescents and many adults have one of these roughly every fifteen minutes.

However, I was an inquisitive child, and my questioning nature was cultivated by my mother. She was a Methodist from Georgia. A southern belle. My father was a Catholic from the lower eastside of New York City. How they met and married could take up its own little book. But they did. And they had me. I am not sure they knew what to do with me. My mother was barely 19 when I was born. My father was 21. But they did their best when it came to religion. My mother had been made to sign a document as a condition of a Roman Catholic church wedding that she would raise her children (me in this case) as Catholic.

I think both she and my father were terrified of my Irish Catholic grandmother who considered my mother a fallen woman. You see, my parents had been married in a civil ceremony and were living as husband and wife without the blessing of the Roman Catholic Church. So, my mother signed the document and, though neither of my parents had what you might have called strong religious feelings, I was dutifully raised as a Catholic boy in what the nuns told us was "the One True Church." I went through the Catholic system of First Communion (with Confession, of course), weekly mass, and Confirmation as a young recruit in the Roman Catholic Army of Christ.

The story might have ended there. But, like many parents of their generation, my parents made the fundamental mistake of introducing a series of parallel, complementary mythologies to what I heard at mass on Sundays.

For example, I was taught to believe in the Divine Rabbit (more commonly known as the Easter Bunny) and to expect from him gift baskets of candy that miraculously appeared in our living room each Easter morning. There was also another minor deity known as the Tooth Fairy. When one of my baby teeth fell out, all I had to do was put it under my pillow and the next morning there would be a bright shiny quarter. Miraculous, right? Then, of course, there was the Big Guy: Santa Claus (also known as Saint Nicholas). We celebrated his feast day every year on December 25. Though they did not call it Santa Claus Day, that is what it seemed to the toy greedy budding pagan that I was. There was much that was wrong and dysfunctional in my family of origin. But my parents, pretty much, did Santa Claus right. There would be lots of presents under the tree. Sometimes these would be what I had asked for. Usually, they would just be gifts appropriate to my age and gender. I believed in the Easter Bunny. I believed in the Tooth Fairy. And I believed in Santa Claus with all my heart.

My pantheon of minor gods first began to fall apart with a realization that the Easter Bunny and the Tooth Fairy were not real. It was not particularly traumatic. It was part of growing up. Maybe I heard something in school or someone in the neighborhood said, "you don't still believe in the Easter Bunny, do you?" Or maybe I realized that the candy baskets that appeared on Easter Bunny Day were identical to the ones I saw sold in the local drug store, cellophane wrapper and all.

But I still believed in Santa Claus. You could not tell me Saint Nick was not real.

He had more credentials. There are songs about him, books, television specials. He keeps a "naughty or nice list" which fit nicely into my growing Catholic guilt. And, to make his bona fides ironclad, I had heard he was also **Saint Nicholas**, a genuine Catholic Saint. In fact, since I was a relatively lazy child, I had been praying my Christmas lists to him from the age of seven. Praying my Christmas list lying comfortably in my bed saved me the effort of laboriously writing a "Dear Santa" note. It even saved me the bother of having to ask my parents for a postage stamp. And didn't the presents always appear, proving I had a direct line?

Then I finally figured out that Santa Claus was simply something I had been good naturedly lied to about by my parents as a kind, loving prank. And my entire mythological edifice began to crumble.

Jesus Christ (like Santa) was also something my parents had told me about and asked me to believe. Why should I trust that belief any more than I trusted the other fantasies I had been told about the Tooth Fairy, the Easter Bunny, and Santa Claus?

I became one of those obnoxious teenagers of the Holden Caulfield variety who saw phoniness everywhere with resistance to anything sounding like religion. I saw only the hypocrisy of religion with the wars fought in its name, sexual abuses by the Catholic clergy and the immense amount of money collected to support the lavish lifestyles of the upper echelons in the church. I came to regard believers as an inferior subset of humanity worthy of contempt or pity depending on my mood. Over recent years especially, I have come to develop an understanding of Jesus Christ (the Son of Man) as an advanced spirit, teacher, and a significant force in our evolution toward God. I believe he set the direction for that evolution when he said, "the Father and I are one" and invited others to adopt this kind of relationship toward God as co-creators and partners. The Jesus Christ that I stopped believing in was that one that I learned had been created by pagan Romans beginning in the first and second century. This was the one the nuns and brothers preached, not the historical man or the great spiritual teacher.

Dropping this belief was no more of a loss than letting go of the Easter Bunny, the Tooth Fairy, or Santa Claus.

It allowed me to open myself to something much more miraculous, deep, and rewarding than the fairytales of my childhood.

Another factor in my development as a budding skeptic was my mother's influence. My mother was never completely onboard with the Roman Catholic faith. Methodists have a simple idea about Christianity – less emphasis on rituals, saints, worship of the Virgin Mary as an auxiliary goddess and none, of course, in the Catholic hierarchy and its traditions. Yet she got stuck serving as my coach for the hours of memorization required to become indoctrinated into the Catholicism that she had been coerced into supporting. And the Catholic religion, at least when I was growing up, was very big on rote memorization of dogma for its youngest members. There was a blue book called *The Baltimore Catechism* that we were supposed to commit to memory. It was basically a series of questions and answers – the penalty for not parroting it back could be a rap on the knuckles by a displeased nun. So, my mother would read me the question. I would try to recite the answer and get it is close to perfect as possible.

She would ask me a question from the book on some issue of Catholic dogma and after I had played back what I thought was the correct answer, I would ask "is that right?" My mother, who had a dour sense of humor and a tendency toward passive aggression, would reply "well, that's what it says **here**." I remember once – and so appreciate this – I asked, "is that right?" My mother said "well, that's what you are SUPPOSED to believe."

I am grateful for my mother's low-key guerilla war against the Catholic Church. I now see all religions as potential pathways to higher understanding and eventually to union with God, but also as potential pitfalls to true spiritual growth. I was fortunate to find a path that simply works for me. And I think you may agree that we all ultimately must find our own path if we are to grow in spiritual understanding. My path just happens to lie well outside a formal religious structure. But I know for many it is within an organized faith. And I know many people who, in maturity, rediscover the beauty of their childhood faith. This is just not my path. Maybe, encouraged by my mother's rebellion against a faith that would have consigned us both to everlasting torment, I am at core a natural inquirer and questioner. I know there are things that I do not know. And I know I have a longing in my heart to know more. This book – *My Autobiographies* – is part of that process. Perhaps it will be part of yours as well: in fact, I hope so.

Somewhere along my journey I became exposed to the doctrine of reincarnation, a commonly accepted notion in many parts of our world. Once I seriously considered reincarnation as a possible explanation for the wonder of human existence, I felt I had no choice but to pursue it for personal development as well as to satisfy a philosophical curiosity. Even during my days struggling with the *Baltimore Catechism*, I had always lived within questions such as "what is it really to be human?" or "what is consciousness anyway?" and an old favorite "do souls survive the body's death?" In my opinion, these are questions each of us must come to terms with to be fully self-actualized and deal with to a greater or lesser extent.

I went through the ordinary stages of growing up: high school, college, discovering my talents and matching those with opportunities I saw, exploring and experiencing sexuality and love, and generally trying to make it in the world. I followed a profession as an advertising writer. I married and had children. I fell into traps of addiction, continuing a family tradition perhaps influenced by my genetic structure. I recovered and started life anew as many like me are blessed to. And then I redefined myself professionally and started a new career in consciousness development and personal growth as a hypnotist and instructor of other hypnotists. But those unanswered questions summarized best perhaps by "what is it all about?" were always in the back of my mind. Like many people, the answers provided by my childhood upbringing and the culture at large did not satisfy this hunger. And so, I began my quest into what I now call *My Autobiographies*.

In this little book, I will relate to you fourteen separate autobiographical snippets that reflect my journey. I will not attempt to decide for you whether these stories are simply fanciful imaginations derived from my subconscious. They may very well be. After all, I already confided to you that I worked as an advertising writer – paid to come up with clever concepts. I will say that each of these experiences seemed, and still seems, authentic. But you will need to be the judge of what they really were. You are certainly welcome to simply read this little book as fiction – a way of me presenting myself to you as well as to myself through these third-party narratives.

It is certainly possible that the stories I will relate to you in this little narration are products of my imagination originating, perhaps from my own psychology and at times I will confess my psychopathology. I accept the scientific method of experimentation and observation but not to the exclusion of flashes of insight and revelation. Yet I cannot deny – and will not under-emphasize – that the experiences I will relate to you seemed real and often had an emotional reality every bit as substantive as any experience I had within what is accepted as our shared consensual reality.

In other words, I know that I have no proof I lived as a soldier in The First Continental Dragoons or a stone age hunter or the mother of three beautiful sons who ran a construction "empire" in the near east or the wife of a blacksmith somewhere in rural Poland or Russia. I cannot prove the validity of any of the experiences I will relate to you. But what I can attest with absolute conviction is that each of these experiences seemed real as I discovered them and that experiencing them provided insight, understanding, and psychic relief that has benefited me in my journey in this life.

So, I ask you, dear reader, to join me in regarding these narrations as phenomena without questioning (at this point at least) too deeply their objective validity. It is my hope that, by relating these stories, you may find yourself wondering whether you yourself could generate your own saga of "autobiographies." I also hope to inspire you to consider that you might just benefit in emotional well-being and personal effectiveness by doing so. So, I guess I do invite you – at least for the moment – to suspend disbelief and just enjoy the journey with me.

And I understand why you might be reluctant to do so.

For example, I personally have trouble relating to people's stories of extraterrestrial abduction. I kind of go blank when someone starts talking about their visit to The Mother Ship. Yet I do not think I am missing much by not following UFO narratives and dwelling on the possibility of visitors from another galaxy. If visitors from outside our solar system really are visiting our planet, surely we will all know one day. I can wait to find out when it is reported on CNN that an ambassador from Alpha Centauri's spaceship has landed on the White House lawn. But I think I do lose something fundamental if I automatically reject the possibility of the doctrine of reincarnation. When someone relates a story about being taken up into a ship by the "grays" and anally probed, the end result (pardon the pun) is simply the possibility that life on other planets not only exists but that visitors are watching. That may be interesting to you. Or it may not. But that is as far as it goes for now. But the individual who takes on the possibility of multiple incarnations and embarks on an exploration of their own "autobiographies" comes back often with insights into their character and psychological makeup that can literally change their lives. For this reason – though I might be skeptical about the verifiable reality of such experiences – I nonetheless look for the truth behind them. I ask myself, what did the "life" I have just experienced learn from their time here and what of that can I bring into my present life? Often, I find the answer is quite a lot in terms of peace of mind, personal effectiveness, or more.

The fundamental principle that most past life journeyers subscribe to is the idea that each life – each incarnation, including the one you are living right now – has within it a central, underlying theme that must be resolved sooner or later. Some might call it a karmic contract. Others might call it a spiritual mission. I like to think about it as a question that must be answered for the soul to go on and graduate to the "next level."

Behind all of this is the notion of spiritual evolution. It has seemed to me for a long time that humanity – you and I – are in the process of growth to becoming what you may one day be an entirely new species. The name I have used for the species in my own musings for well over 30 years has been HomoDeus. GodMan. It seems to me that the destiny of humanity is to move closer and closer to our Creator. It is not my intention to go too deeply into this – partly for the desire not to appear overly grandiose – but also so as not to alienate you, dear reader. Whether you believe in reincarnation or are even willing to consider the possibility that humanity is in the process of evolution, I hope will be irrelevant to your enjoyment of these stories or seeing whether my experiences might be something you could apply to your own life.

But perhaps I really have deviated too far from my main story and I ask your indulgence.

You will notice that I am occasionally allow these "lives" to speak more directly to you in short blank verse "poems." I do not pretend there is much artistry in these efforts – you might call them "screams of consciousness." I found the loose format allowed the lives speak to you with less of my ordinary conscious mind filter. My past lives themselves seemed to demand this method of expression.

The actual method of past-life access varies from practitioner to practitioner. But the typical past-life journey follows a standard pattern. A hypnotic induction begins the process. Your practitioner will guide you into trance by lulling your conscious, analytical mind into a "sleep." I put sleep in quotation marks because you will be aware of what is going on but feel a sense of distance from your regular mental processes. Additionally, the practitioner will start to directly address parts of yourself that are ordinarily below the level of conscious thought. A definition of hypnosis, in fact, is the bypass of the conscious analytical mind to address the subconscious directly. An easy way to think about the hypnotic trance is as a state between dreaming and being in normal waking consciousness. Once you have achieved a good level of trance, the practitioner will use some method to guide your imagination past your birth into some kind of neutral zone. From here, you will be guided into whatever past life experience your subconscious – or perhaps soul – wishes you to explore. Typically, the practitioner will ask you questions during this phase of the session which may last just a few minutes or an hour or even longer. He or she will ask you to report on your gender, emotions, clothing style, whether you are alone or with people, and similar questions. The practitioner will ask you questions about the events you describe and urge you to work through emotions and eventually move toward experiences in this life that are significant. The process can become quite emotional as you relive past trauma. There are also two ways you may be directed in this part of the process. Your practitioner may direct you to speak to him or her from the persona of the life you are visiting in the first-person voice. Or he or she may simply ask you to report on what is happening as an observer. Often the experience is emotionally draining. There may be tears as old loses are revisited, but also moments of joy.

So, now that you have some background....

LET 'S BEGIN
AT THE END:
MY END

The end of my current life seems like a very logical place to begin for a narrative that may stretch the reader's conception of time.

It was the fall of 2019. I had signed up to attend a training in Santa Rosa, California to become a past life hypnotist. Despite the fact that I had conducted dozens of past-life sessions with clients, it seemed wise to get some specific training if only to validate the work I was already doing. The weekend before I was scheduled to leave for the west coast, I had been invited to speak at a conference of alternative healers in Rhode Island. The attendees included traditional people from the world of psychotherapy, but also explorers in other modalities such as reiki and shamanism. After I delivered my talk, I lingered at the event to attend a workshop delivered by a Native American shaman. She was a very impressive woman who also was a registered nurse and a professor of nursing at a local university.

She invited us that afternoon to experience our own death.

Now, that may not sound particularly appealing to you, but as she explained, it was a way of freeing you from attachment to this life. I was intrigued and signed up on the spot. She had us close our eyes (of course). Then she began to chat and drum. But before we got into this state of meditational focus, she talked at some length about the spiritual journey after death. Those who have read the books I mentioned earlier are familiar with the idea that after death there is a journey into the spiritual realms. Generally, those who experience this journey describe it as a time of reflection in which one comes to terms with one's life.

Often, people who have been in these near-death experiences will say that they encounter relatives, spiritual iconic figures, or other guides who help them on their way. The speaker talked a little bit about those spirits who do not quickly graduate, the earthbound ones – the ones we might call ghosts.

We began the journey. Chanting. Drumming. I felt myself entering a state of what I am comfortable calling trance. But I was not moving anywhere in my journey toward "The Light." I was stuck in darkness and I found myself thinking that perhaps at the end of my life I will be one of those creatures who are stuck and doomed to wander the Earth. She had said that those who are stuck in this manner are held back by unresolved issues. These might include deep resentments or unsettled business. So, I was not particularly happy about the experience – I felt others were probably already up amongst the angelic choirs while I was stumbling around in this very dark place. Eventually, I felt the presence of positive angelic forces and I began to gradually trudge my way up to join my spiritual family. Then I felt an overpowering emotion, very powerful: anger, even rage. The shaman facilitator had talked about how some souls get stuck on the way back to the Source. I was beginning to think that perhaps I will be one of them. And then I bumped into another stuck spirit: the spirit of my recently deceased father. He was stuck and he was blocking my path. My father and I had never had what you might call a good relationship. I had always felt that I was a disappointment to my father.

My father wanted me to be a boy more like him. Athletic. Devil-may-care. And he had no reservations about letting me know. There was no physical abuse but, from the earliest I can recall, my father maintained a campaign of psychological attack often fueled by his drinking, including blackouts and hangovers. He would ask me questions with imbedded implications. Two of my Dad's favorite questions for his son were "why do you have no commonsense?" and "why can't you do anything right?" My many shortcomings were everyday topics at the dinner table because we were one of those families that often ate the evening meal together. Family time. Of course, there were also the direct attacks where he defined me as a "phony," someone who did not know what he was talking about and, of course, somehow a lesser being.

Accepting his authority as my father, I would contemplate these questions.

When angry, my father occasionally said he was going to kill me. In fairness, it was a different era and I think people were less mindful of the impact of the words they used than hopefully most parents are today. But in my working-class neighborhood, many of the fathers (and some of the mothers) spoke this way. They had been children who grew up in the depression. Many of the men had gone off to fight World War II. Ironically, they were trying to build a better life for their children yet often they seemed to bitterly resent us for being "spoiled" and benefiting from the better life they claimed to want to provide.

Often when I am leading groups, I will ask who in the group did not come from a dysfunctional family. In a group of 30 people I might get one or two raised hands. Most of us in America feel we got off to a bad start in our family of origin. I am no exception; though I will say that I believe being raised in this way is no excuse for how we turn out.

Still, through words and deeds my father gave me the impression that I was unacceptable as a son and a grave disappointment as a potential man. My father liked sports. He liked sports **a lot**. He was a passionate football fan and had been an amateur boxer in his younger years. A bookish, daydreaming, mildly poetic boy was not what he had in mind. So, our relationship was not a happy one and I had the experience (which I have heard many others replicate) that I was simply not "good enough" and fundamentally less worthy than others. This became a central part of my personality. Consequently, as much as I feared my father, I also hated him for his rejection of me and for the way I felt he made me feel.

When I met him blocking my passage to "The Light" in my imagined journey of my passage from this life at that conference in Exeter, Rhode Island, I was furious. My father and I had it out on the spot in some astral plane back alley. He matched my anger with his own. I matched his rage with my own. Finally, I heard myself saying, "what do you want me to say - that I hate myself? Okay, I will say it. *I Hate Myself*. Are you happy now?"

Suddenly, the energy changed completely between us. My father's rage and my own evaporated. In the quiet that followed, I felt him say, "I had no idea." I felt his realization and remorse. It was remorse at the lost possibility of a loving, supportive relationship between us as well as the damage his attitude had done to his son. And I understood at that moment that he had been tough on me because he thought I needed to be like him to survive in the world. I got that he was afraid for me and wanted me to be the kind of hard man that he was. My father did not understand how someone like me – bookish, sensitive, and imaginative – could survive, much less succeed in life. At that point, everything changed between us. Over the years, I had done the kind of work people do in forgiveness regarding my father with some results. I had worked to see life from his point of view – the point of view of a man whose own father had died when he was 12 who had to fight to make it on his own against a world he perceived as hostile. But in this moment, everything changed. I felt love for my father, and I believe, in that instant, wherever his soul was it was released as well.

Together, arm in arm, this man whom I had cordially despised and I continued toward the light in love and partnership. It was amazing and I cannot possibly communicate to you, dear reader, the emotion of that moment of transformation. Along the way, we met another soul who had lost its way and was trapped: the soul of my mother who herself had also recently passed. My mother had a hard life. She suffered from depression and a feeling that life was beyond her control. I believe my mother was disappointed in life. Her one accomplishment and only true joy in life was her children. I have three brothers. But other than us, there was not much for her. My mother often was confused and that is how we found her: confused and anxious after death, as she had often been in life. I had been with my mother when she died; my mother did not know when my father and I met her in the foothills of the world of the spirit that she was deceased. She knew she was lost but not that she was no longer in her body. My father and I patiently explained to her what happened and gave her the good news that we were going to move on to whatever it is that is next. And, as a family, the three of us – once uncomfortable with each other – went together in harmony toward the light.

This was not what I was expecting that afternoon when I simply hung around the conference because I was already there. But, when I think about that moment, I believe there was a kind of divine serendipity that occurred that day. This is something I experience in life from time to time. I think many of us – perhaps you – have had that experience. Things seem to happen in a way that appears to be magical or even miraculous. People call you on the phone when you were thinking about them. Things work out in a particular way that after the fact seems destined or like divine intervention. These things do occur.

I have no specific religion or even theology other than a working understanding of these matters I will write about. But I do think that Whatever Creates All This is guiding us toward something better.

As I mentioned, I have had the thought for many years that humanity is in the process of evolution into something akin to a new species. Some years ago, in meditation, the name of this new species came to my mind: HomoDeus. Our ancestors and ourselves had a good run as homo sapiens (thinking man), but I believe now at this point in history we are evolving into a kind of consciousness that is more in alignment and connected with deity – literally a new species. Some of us – perhaps you – are called upon to be part of that mission.

I am not going to try to draw a physical picture of this new species. I have no opinion as to whether we will have less hair, be less or more androgynous, taller, shorter, lighter, or darker. I believe the important difference will be a newly developed direct connection to the Creator of All of This: God if it is helpful for you to think about IT in a traditional context. Likely, there will be enhanced psychic abilities such telepathy, psychic healing and perhaps some touch of clairvoyance and maybe even psychokinesis. It has occurred to me that the historic Jesus Christ may have been one of the first of this new breed though, obviously, that did not turn out too well for him. The old species, I suspect, rarely welcomes their replacement with open arms.

So, I suppose, more than simply telling my stories, this little book is dedicated to that work. And I do believe it requires more than one life for an individual soul to learn enough to make a meaningful contribution. The Christian perspective that I was introduced to as a Roman Catholic presented the idea that each of us gets only one life. In this one-shot paradigm, you either win or lose. You die and are judged based on how well you have done in the years between your birth and death. You either go to heaven or the other place. One shot. No do-overs. That perspective does not allow for evolution. It is a series of disconnected experiments in consciousness, morality, ethics, altruism, spiritual connection to God that does not go anywhere. It ends with death and judgment.

As I mentioned earlier and I am sure you know, a huge percentage of humanity believes that reincarnation is our shared reality. Once I accepted this belief thoroughly – and had the experiences I will relate to you – I began to see my life as an opportunity for growth rather than as something to be overcome or endured and to appreciate the temporary nature of all life. If you have read this far, this perspective is likely not alien to you. You may already be a believer or, at least, you are likely curious about this way of looking at life.

To get the most from this little book, I invite you to look at your current life as a story, a narrative. But your current life story is simply a chapter in the bigger story of your personal development and the even bigger story of the evolution of humanity itself. I hope you find some peace in this perspective – that it takes some of the tension off living and provides a perspective on how to live.

My sense in these stories and in general is that each life has at least one central mission: a theme. Like a work of fiction, your stories have characters and events. There is a plot. There is a vocabulary. This little book is about your life (and lives) and their theme: **_your central challenge in your current life_**.

By doing past life explorations I have investigated different parts of my persona. I have reached an understanding of myself and my mission here on planet Earth. And I have done it at a greater level of depth than I believe I would ever have achieved through psychotherapy or by following a formalized, rigid religious structure. I see my life (my lives) as a work(s) in progress and there is great joy in that.

I invite you to join me in this journey. Let me start by a "scream of conscious-ness" that comes from my current incarnation: New York City, Caucasian male, 1948 to present.

Like Father – Like Son?
....

Adolph Hitler was
Dictator of the Year
on the cover of TIME Magazine
the Day my Grandfather Died

Leaving my Dad
Man of the House
Twelve-year-old boy
Cold water flat
broke in the
East side of New York
With a mother to support

I never knew if my grandfather
played ball with my Dad
in an empty lot off Canal
or Delancey
Or hugged him when
he skinned his knee
Or read him bedtime stories

But I suspect not

I do not know whether he liked my father
Loved him
Wanted him to be the very best
or was completely absorbed
alone in some addictive hell

I simply do not know.
Or why my father's spirit
chose him to be his Dad
or why my father's spirit chose me to be

After all, I always thought he wanted to me to be other
than what I am - to be like him

A hard man
Football player
Troublemaker
A man among men

Is that what grandfather
wanted from my father
so he became like him?

Would he have been proud of my Dad?

I know I was not what my father had in mind
when he told his friends that night
that his wife had given him a son
handed out cigars
puffed up and proud

He said one drunken day
that I thought
I was Jesus Christ
but since he
made me
that made HIM GOD THE FATHER
"Ha" he laughed
and poked me in the chest

There may have been
some truth in that
Like a grain of sand inside its shell
Irritates an oyster to create a pearl
my father gave me something
against which to stand.

I know he did his best
with what he had in hand:
Me, a timid
bookish kid
who would rather play with girls
than rough and tumble
the way he did

He told me once that he was ashamed of me.
Was it because putting me down
pulled him up in a way he needed
because he felt less
than he thought a man should be?
Or his father thought a man should be?

Yet - and how odd this may sound –
I always knew he
was there for me
a fundamental parent/child loyalty
And when we met on the astral plain
on our way to the light
Two spirits growing in love
connected by a common flight

I saw why I chose him
to be my teacher and my guide
to dance the dance of incarnation -
stumbling sometimes - often blind
arm and arm on our journey
toward the Divine.

Today I can honor my father
my Teacher
my Father
My Friend

An independent man
Burdened down by
the chip on his shoulder
but I am proud to say
unbroken until the end

We will get back to my current life story later in this little book. But for right now please join me about 200 years ago as a sad sack soldier in the First Continental Dragoons: Private Reilly.

PRIVATE REILLY
THE MAN WITH THE SILK SHIRT LIKE SOME OF THE OFFICERS

(UNITED STATES – LATE 18TH CENTURY)

I am not quite sure why I first became drawn to the investigation of my past lives. But I began this journey twenty years ago. A woman came into my life who was a past life therapist. At the time, she was practicing in my home state of Rhode Island. I had experience with hypnotism and had been trained as a hypnotist in my late 20s so the idea of hypnotic regression was familiar to me. I scheduled a session with her purely on impulse. In the world of the spirit, it is useful to adopt the perspective that "there are no such things as coincidences." For example, somehow this book got into your hands. What you do with this information is up to you. But it might be useful to consider that coming across this book is not accidental. Perhaps, connecting with these stories is meant to be a part of your spiritual growth, maybe even an important part. After the hypnotic induction, I was guided to a place between lives as the jumping off point. Then suddenly, I found myself meeting the character that identified itself as Private Reilly. To my surprise, I found myself almost literally becoming Reilly. He was talking with the therapist through my mouth and words. As I – or I should say Private Reilly – started talking to the past life therapist, I began to vividly experience images from a different time and personality. I felt my lips curling because I started to introduce myself as Corporal Reilly. It was only with some reluctance that I corrected to my actual rank as **Private** Reilly.

I "met" Private Reilly at a time of great emotional stress. Reilly was – it is fair to say – a pretentious little man. He was a private (not a corporal) in, I believe, the First Continental Dragoons during the Revolutionary War. One of Reilly's pretensions was that he owned a silk shirt like those that some of the officers wore on special occasions. Not a homespun shirt, but a silk shirt. I suppose you could call Reilly a social climber. I am not sure about his family background. The session did not reveal that information. I suppose I can go back and try to reconnect with the Reilly Energy. But the emotional truth was that Reilly had a chip on his shoulder and felt fundamentally inferior. I have come to understand that people who need to be well thought of – look for their validity from outside sources – are at core plagued with feelings of inadequacy. I am sure Reilly was in that category: a man who felt the world did not appreciate his fine qualities of leadership, intellect, and character.

It was night in Reilly's world when I met him and he was on a mission. Reilly's assignment was to deliver a written message to his captain at a function in a fine house. I am not sure whether it was a festive ball or a meeting of officers in the evening. But Reilly, in his silk shirt, felt filled with self-importance. He goes up to the front door – not the back – and tells the soldier at the door that he must come in to give his captain an important message. Whoever it was at the door was not impressed. He told Reilly to wait in the foyer. He would personally hand the message to the captain.

One of the characteristics of past life regression work is that sometimes details at first seem confused but if you are open and patient they gradually become clear. But as soon as I entered the home I realized something was off with the lights. In my entire life, I have never been in a large room entirely lit by candles. The illumination in the large, candle-lit ballroom I peered into was different from anything I had ever experienced. This kind of detail has made me open to the possibility that these experiences are not simple replays of television or movie images. They seem more like recollections than creations.

Reilly protests weakly, but then the message is taken from his hand and delivered presumably to Reilly's captain. This was not Reilly's mission. Reilly was clear that he had been commissioned to hand the message to his captain.

That is what he had been told to do and what he envisioned doing. That this was not happening threw Reilly into a tailspin. Reilly leaves that large, stately home crestfallen and despondent. He is upset. His self-esteem has taken a major whack. He goes to a pub to drown his sorrows. I experience being at this pub. Reilly has a large tankard of ale and he is miserable and very confused. He feels utterly defeated. Reilly imagines going back to his unit and explaining that he had failed to deliver the important message as ordered. He is afraid of what people will think of him.

Suddenly, something happens with a BANG.

Another aspect of past life work is the importance of accepting whatever comes up without judgment. Perhaps Reilly was shot in the back of the head for some reason. Perhaps Reilly had a brain aneurysm. All I know is that I felt my consciousness shoot up through the three stories of the pub. BANG. BANG. BANG. I experienced my consciousness being shot out of the pub into the cosmos. And that is how Reilly's life ends.

When I thought about what I had experienced it seemed very vivid. It also seemed important. What happened to Reilly that day was to get trapped in an emotional firestorm. He was highly upset when he died and Reilly left that life with unresolved emotions. He was a little man in the eyes of society. He faced it at his death and found it intolerable. My takeaway from Reilly's life was awareness of my own lifelong battle with needing to be validated by other people's opinion of me. The question Reilly left that life with – his karmic question – was how can I make people treat me well, how can I be seen as important, and why do people not treat me as the great man I fantasize myself to be?

When I think of my various explorations – *My Autobiographies* – my life as Private Reilly seems central to my current situation. It began a revolution in my psychic and leaves me feeling significantly more comfortable just being myself.

It also started me on the journey that led to this book.

Private Confusion
....

I would have been a leader of men
if people would only let me
But seems I am invisible
Barely here – barely there

Not well-born
Or especially strong
Though Caesar Himself
Was just a little man
And people saw him
so powerful his vision
shaped his world

Why does no one see
the great within me?
Why do they ignore
the greatness only I can see?

Why should I not
hate them all?
The stern-faced men
the smiley ones
the ones others naturally
look to for guidance
naturally obey?
Why not me?

Was I born to be invisible?
A shade living – yet undead –
that cannot make itself heard
no matter how loud I rattle my invisible chains?

I should have been put in charge
I should have been
The One who says
this one should go
that one must stay

But they speak to me
through me
like speaking through thin air
and yet accuse me of arrogance
putting on airs

Could it be that
jealousy makes them
leery of me?
Or selfishness makes
them horde
all the power and glory
for themselves?

Or do they simply
know some arcane
secret kept from me mischievously?

Or am I really
just a little man
obscurity my fate?

Maybe one day
they will come
and place me high
until then I suffer
unseen
wondering why
why not me?

And that is Reilly's story: the story of a little man with delusions of grandeur and a silk shirt meant to show the world who he wanted people to think himself to be.

Next is a man who knew exactly who he was in reality but had questions about the nature of reality itself.

THE MAN
WHO TRIED TO GET POWER FROM A RHINOSAURES

(AFRICA BEFORE CONTACT WITH EUROPEANS)

I could have started "my autobiographies" with this man because he is the one I most identify with in my current life.

He was a shaman – a medicine man – an important man to his tribe. The year? I have no idea though it was certainly before the indigenous population of Africa became corrupted through contact with missionaries and European civilization, technology, and ideas.

I first met this shaman when he was officiating at a tribal ceremony. He was dressed in feathers and furs. He wore colorful carvings and beads. He had an elaborate mask of either a demon or God. I am not sure which and not sure he knew either. He had a rattle that he sounded to a beat synchronized by the stomping and clapping of the tribe assembled in the central square of the village. He had fringes of animal hair around his ankles and arms. His face under the mask was also painted as were his arms, legs, and torso. He was a sight to behold. Impressive. But when I first met him, I experienced him from the inside. I knew that no matter how impressive and convincing he was to others it was quite a different story on the inside. Within him beat the heart of an inquirer and even a skeptic. He did every single ritual to the best of his ability. Perfectly, in fact. All the right herbs, dance steps, and ornaments. He was his tribe's connection with the gods and spirits upon whom the village depended for protection and sometimes survival. But, despite the fact that he took his role very, very seriously, he was never really certain if any of the things he did made a difference to the tribe's well-being.

It was not that he was cynical or even especially disillusioned. He was not. It was not that he was a fraud. He was not. He did the best he could as he had been trained by those before him. They, in turn, had been trained by those before them. He was the Shaman, the village spiritual leader. He took his role as gate-keep between the world of the seen and the unseen world of spirit very seriously. I was conscious as I met him that he considered his position in the tribe a sacred trust.

I received glimpses of him in the huts of the village working his magic with frightened villagers when children or elders were ill. I saw him at the height of his glory when the chief of the tribe had come down with an inexplicable ailment. I watched him pull out all the stops. He carefully chose the right dance moves, the right smoke from certain herbs and the best chants for an unexplained illness. And when, as if by magic, the chief recovered, I felt his joy at the chief's miraculous recovery. But I was acutely aware that this joyful emotion was felt side-by-side with his questioning whether anything he did had contributed to this happy result.

Sometimes he would say to those of the villagers who were interested in such things that "there are things in the world that are known and there are things in this world that are unknown. My journey is to walk between these worlds and guide you to avoid traps on both sides." He was not an arrogant man. Very much the contrary, he was a seeker who did his best to walk between these two worlds because both were real to him. He felt he had an intimate relationship with the spirits that were in charge of the local streams and forests as well as the greater gods that made the clouds move through the sky and the sun rise and fall. He knew and respected the power of the evil ones who lurked in the shadows each dusk and ruled through the night. I recalled vividly a relationship he cultivated with an ancient, gnarled tree. It was in a little clearing away from the village. It was a far enough walk that the villagers would not likely visit. To my surprise, I came to realize that this special tree was his confidant. He would pose questions to the tree and listen for its wisdom – roots gripped into the rich soil. He would wait and answers would come. Sometimes, they would burst into his awareness vividly. Sometimes, they would be whispers. It was easy for him to trust the loud voices. Do this. Do that. Do not do this. Do not do that. But whether they were whispery or insistent, he was never quite sure if they were simply ruminations from his own mind. This is the kind of man he was.

He was a searcher and questioner. The universe, creation, even consciousness itself fascinated him.

And, so it went on, year after year. A life well-lived. But no one gets out of any life without **drama** and **trauma**. And these moments of drama and trauma, of intense emotion, are often related to the central themes of a life – karmic missions if you will. In my shaman's case, he had long been obsessed with the power of the rhinoceros. I sensed clearly that this was his totem spirit animal. He knew that powdered rhinoceros' horns were good for many ailments. These included restoring a man's sexual potency, curing fainting fevers, and even giving a dying man a second chance at life. He knew there was powerful magic in the horn of a rhino. He had begun to wonder whether it would be possible to absorb the rhino's power through chant and communion with the animal's spirit itself. If he could merge with the rhino that generated all this power, perhaps he could take that power into himself and become as powerful as a rhino. It seemed as he obsessed about the project that power, wisdom, and magical transformation were all within reach behind the rhino's steely gaze.

This is how he died one oppressively hot afternoon. He was not fully dressed in ceremonial garb. He only wore a few strategic decorations. He carried a special rattle prepared for the occasion.

I do not believe he had consulted with the wise tree on this plan. If he had, like many people who seek advice but really want their own decision validated, I suspect he would have found a way to ignore any advice against such a foolish undertaking. My shaman felt he must find what lay on the other side of this experiment.

So, my shaman tried to stare down a neighborhood rhino and mesmerize him for lack of a better word. The idea seemed to be to join spirits with the rhino and thereby share its power. This was a rhino that had been showing up at odd times when the shaman was walking alone looking for herbs. The night before he did the fateful experiment, he had dreamt he was riding on the rhino's back. This seemed a clear omen if ever there was one. He told no one in the village of his plan. But this was not unusual. He had been in the habit of keeping his own counsel for his entire life.

The experiment did not go well.

My shaman died that day, gorged by 3000 pounds of muscle and outrage that this strange painted, feathered man had dared to try to take the rhino's power for himself.

It did not seem that my shaman was greedy or power mad. I do not think he was trying to defeat the rhino. He was simply curious. And that is the quality I love most about this life: curiosity. My shaman lived in the line between two worlds: between the world of the known and the world of the unknown. But his heart dwelt often in its own world: wonderment and awe at the very mystery and majesty of creation.

He was a beautiful man. A humble man. And he was an engaged, curious soul. Of all the incarnations that I have been privileged to experience, his is the one that does me the most honor and whose recollection gives me the most pleasure and joy.

My legacy in this life – as a hypnotist and coach of people – is to follow in his footsteps. Though, this time, I will try to avoid experiments as risky as gleaning power from a rhinoceros. I may be a slow learner. But this lesson would be a hard one to forget and I doubt I will ever be tempted to stare down a 3000-pound wild animal in my current life.

If every life is designed to explore a question (and I believe each is), the Shaman's mission was to formulate deeper and better questions until he found ultimate truth. His message to me is to keep questioning. My quest in this life is and always has been a search the true nature of reality and, yes, to tap its power, not just for me but for others, perhaps even you as you read these stories.

But I also believe – and I think my shaman would agree with me – that there is as much (if not more) power in the simple act of questioning as in the answers themselves.

Rhino Power

I do not know what I am doing
But I do it well
Like my father and his before
A Shaman – a Magic Man

I communicate with the spirts
and all the gods
I chant the chants
Work my rattles
Wave my rod
I apply the right herbs
and read the entrails of frogs
I know when seasons change
And when planting is right
when sacrifices must be made
and harvest is ripe

I do not know why I do
what I do, but I do it well

When you are sick
you call me and I come ready
with spells, potions
accompanied by a host of spirits and Gods

I mark the magic marks
chant the magic words
and when you recover
I am amazed along with you

and wonder
what it was I did that scared
out the bad
and brought in the good

I help you move to
the other side
when it is your time to move on.
And when you are gone
I ponder with your family
what evil spirit was the cause
of your demise

My totem is the rhino
for I, like him,
am steady and strong
when I am focused
I charge in a rhino trance
of perfect concentration focus

Head down
Horn up

And this is how I die
Focused head down
Trying to get power from a Rhino

It is when I finally realize
I do not know what I am doing
Though I do it very well

As a Rhino
gorges a humble, foolish
Magic Man
into his next life
with the power of
his Rhino Horn

The next life I will share with you was that of another spiritual seeker but in this life my soul had a radically different theology. This incarnation had much less curiosity but was afflicted with an unfortunate certainty that ended up causing its death.

BROTHER
THOMAS

(GERMANY, NEAR COLOGNE – 15ᵀᴴ CENTURY)

Suicide may or may not be a sin: but it is never a good idea karmically. Like they say, "suicide is a permanent solution to a temporary problem." What they do not say is that the repercussions can go on for many lifetimes until the problem that called for a temporary solution is finally faced and resolved.

I will never be clear how much of my tendency to be thin-skinned comes from my biology, my early upbringing, or the life of Brother Thomas. Maybe all three sources contributed to what my family called my tendency to "overreact" to criticism. But I believe, if any of these reincarnation experiences are valid, that a lot of it came from my life as a medieval cleric with a rather large chip on his shoulder that ended up causing his demise. His name was Brother Thomas – a Christian scholar and monk in 15ᵗʰ century Cologne, Germany. Impressive credentials. A man of God. But my legacy from Brother Thomas was far less about spirituality than about egotism, fear, and confusion. I believe these traits may have been locked into my soul at the time of his death by hanging himself from a tree a hundred yards from the monastery walls.

Brother Thomas, you see, took his own life at a time of extreme emotional distress originating from what he perceived of as an attack against his integrity and spiritual authority. Let me emphasize again that I have been oversensitive to people's opinions of me for my whole life. In fact, ironically, I have been severely criticized for being overly sensitive to criticism because, at times, criticism has made me go more than a little crazy. A psychologist or well-meaning therapist would, no doubt, attribute my delicate sensibilities on this issue to a troubled childhood with a hyper-critical father. My father went out of his way at virtually every opportunity to point out my inadequacies. My father was an active alcoholic until my junior year of college. He also had suffered through an exceedingly difficult early life. As I mentioned earlier, my father's own father had died when he was 12. So, even though my father was highly intelligent, he ended up going to work full-time at an early age – never graduated high school – and did not really come into his own until he found sobriety in his 40s.

Given all this, you don't need an education in psychology to think, "Well, this makes perfect sense. As a result of upbringing in a dysfunctional alcoholic family, you became hypersensitive. This leads to a textbook adulthood as an Adult Child of An Alcoholic." Simple as that.

But my exploration of past lives has opened for me another possibility: Brother Thomas and my life as a 15th century academic monk and teacher near Cologne, Germany who took his own life essentially due to over-sensitivity fueled by grandiosity.

Whether this prior life experience was a contributing factor – or simply an explanatory story my subconscious mind weaved to make sense myself – I do not know. Frankly, my mind is open on the subject.

What had me seek out this particular past life experience was a bad social media review. As a practicing hypnotist, I depend on reviews, recommendations, and referrals to maintain my business. One day, I received a particularly vicious social media review from a woman I had never worked with but said I was obviously a horrible hypnotist. She said this based on an error in scheduling not any work with her as a client. I should have just let it go. Instead, I tried to appeal to her sense of fairness to modify her review and offered to work with her at no cost to make amends for any inconvenience. She escalated her attacks. I was beside myself with upset. I recognized that my reaction was over and above what the situation warranted. But that knowledge didn't help. I spoke with friends about the incident. That didn't help. Eventually, I contacted a past life therapist and set to work investigating whether a karmic hiccup could be contributing to my overreaction.

Here is the story as it revealed itself to me.

I found myself as Brother Thomas in his private residence. His comfortable room was in a turret located in what I assumed to be a monastery, a local center of learning. I saw Brother Thomas surrounded by manuscripts and books. He was a teacher of theology, philosophy, and canon law. He loved everything about his life. I was filled with a sense of incredible self-satisfaction and peace. I did not know Brother Thomas' socio-economic background. I suspected he may have been from the artisan or small tradesmen class. His origins were humble but not the very bottom of society. I was sure Brother Thomas saw the church as a chance for advancement and a pleasant life. But more than the status and comforts it offered, he loved the life itself. He loved ideas, concepts, and learning. He also enjoyed pontificating (though he would have called it teaching or spreading knowledge). If ever there was a man content in his own company – with his own ideas – who felt his world made perfect sense – it was Brother Thomas.

His classroom was down a flight of stone stairs from his pleasant rooms in the turret. His life and his work were intertwined physically as well as emotionally. When I walked down to my classroom as Brother Thomas, I felt his stocking-less feet encased in rough sandals and the reassuring weight of his heavy, woolen clerical garb. I graciously greeted my nine students. These young men had been waiting patiently for my entrance. Brother Thomas basked in their approval. But, as you will discover in past life exploration (or already have in this life), nobody gets out of any life without some pain. Hopefully, you will also learn that behind the pain there is always a lesson. Though it must be said that knowing there is a lesson hidden within the pain doesn't necessarily make it any less painful.

As I mentioned, what led me to the past life exploration that led me to Brother Thomas was a criticism of my professionalism and a personal attack against my character. I felt the attack was completely unfair. But I could not get this individual out of my mind. Her public criticism was literally the first thing

I thought of upon awakening and often my last thought before I fell asleep. I ruminated over and over on the exact wording that she had used. I would craft powerful counter arguments. I imagined publishing these to get people on my side and discredit her. I got to the point where I had to do something to alter my obsession for my own mental health.

I met with the past life therapist and quickly went into trance. And I met Brother Thomas. He was not only a kindred soul, but I imagine my soul in a prior life. I experienced how his life changed utterly one fateful day when a new student joined Brother Thomas' class. This student did not want to be there studying theology, church law, and scripture. He was a nobleman, and such things were beneath him. I believed he may already have held a rank above that of a simple priest or friar despite his youth and lack of training. To compound the issue, the young man was the Archbishop's "nephew" which was code in those times for illegitimate son. This young man was taking Brother Thomas' class only as a required step to his eventual elevation to greater honors. He had no interest in the subject matter. The church for him was simply a way to enjoy a lavish lifestyle and build a high-profile career. I know that. Anyone observing the situation would know that. Brother Thomas did not see it that way.

One of the things about past life work – if it is to be effective – is the past life voyager must be willing to experience the emotions that go along with the lesson that each life offers. And Brother Thomas was upset to the point of insanity over this young man. The nobleman did not want to be in Brother Thomas' class. Likely, he had zero interest in the day-to-day of a religious life. His attitude toward Thomas was dismissive and irreverent. He thought Brother Thomas, the class itself, and all that went into a clerical life absurd and, worse yet for a young man of his class, boring. He was young and ambitious. The religious life was simply what a young nobleman without property had to do to get ahead. Like many of his social class pushed into a religious life, the young nobleman's career goal was to become a "prince of the church." He had no interest in piety or learning. He wanted girls, drink, good times, and wealth to afford them. He knew that in the corrupt system of the pre-reformation times he could find all this following his father's path. But first he had to graduate from Brother Thomas' class in ecclesiastical law.

| 49

Brother Thomas did not understand or accept this reality. He felt his outrage as intense emotional agony and even a physical pain at times. Upon awakening, the unfairness of this young man's presence in his sacred classroom was the first thing Thomas thought of. Often, it was his last thought before sleep. The idea that Thomas was expected to be deferential to this privileged child was anathema to everything of which the learned friar thought he stood. He spent his day ruminating over the issue. He would mentally state and then re-state his case to himself and sometimes to others. To Brother Thomas, it seemed clear that any reasonable person would share his outrage at this indignity. He had no doubt that any rational Christian who heard this story would know this was very, very wrong and that something must be done to correct the situation as quickly as possible for the sake of Mother Church Herself.

This mental and emotional storm brewed daily in the cleric's mind for several weeks. It built and built. It grew hotter and hotter. And then there were incidents – certain days in class when the young man said something that especially wounded Brother Thomas' ego. These days, Brother Thomas could not sleep at night but paced around and around his turret.

You get the picture.

One day, Brother Thomas confided his concern and upset to his mentor: the monastery's abbot. It is likely he and the abbot had been friends since Thomas joined the monastery as an acolyte. He was a man whom Brother Thomas trusted absolutely and whom Thomas regarded as a genuine man of God. He told the good abbot the story of this horrible young man. He tried to enlist the abbot's help in asserting discipline or perhaps even removing the young man from the course of study. I do not know whether the abbot tried to calm Brother Thomas down and help Thomas de-escalate the issue or not. It is possible that Brother Thomas had completely misjudged the character of his older friend and the abbot had always been deep under the control of the local church hierarchy. But whatever happened during their conversation, the abbot's response was to take Thomas' complaint to the Archbishop of the district: the boy's "uncle." The situation went from bad to much, much worse.

The 13th, 14th, and 15th centuries were not an era the Roman Catholic Church is particularly proud of. The church was notoriously corrupt. Tickets to heaven (absolutions and indulgences) were routinely sold. There was no separation between church and state. High church offices went to nobility and aristocracy. The peasants paid the price. The princes of the church lived like princes indeed. They had girlfriends, wives, and led lavish lifestyles. And they had children. It was common practice amongst these men to refer to their bastard sons as their nephews.

I do not know if Thomas' naivete was so extreme that he was unaware that the Archbishop was the young man's father not his uncle. More likely, as the true believer he was, Thomas believed that the principles of canon law were so powerful they would show themselves superior to the self-interest of the powerful. But nonetheless, he found himself called on the carpet before the Archbishop who was outraged that Brother Thomas (a lowly cleric) had disrespected his "nephew."

In the Archbishop's palace, I felt myself in Brother Thomas' shoes as he trembled during his interview with the powerful lord. I cringed as I was asked an important question, "who do you think you are?" In my current incarnation this was often a question that my own father would ask me and I would have great trouble answering without offending him. I bring this up now because I can never be sure whether my subconscious invented Brother Thomas or whether a genuine prior life experience as Brother Thomas set the stage for my childhood experience. You, my dear reader, are welcome, of course, to form your own opinion about my story or, if you investigate them, your own autobiographies. But I do know in that moment as Brother Thomas I felt completely destroyed and it seemed very real. This encounter with the Archbishop destroyed Thomas' world and sense of self identity. He was shattered. He felt like nothing and nobody. Back in the monastery, they took away his class and his comfortable, cozy turret and bedroom/study. He was assigned to the kitchen.

My next experience of Brother Thomas was of him in the kitchen peeling potatoes. Emotionally, he is empty, a broken man. There is one poignant moment when the young noble man and some of his friends amuse themselves by visiting the kitchen. They enjoy a good laugh and make sport of the self-satisfied professor, now the kitchen scullery maid. But Brother Thomas is so bereft he gives them little satisfaction: he simply does not care. He is dead inside.

As I mentioned, it is often said that suicide is a permanent solution to a temporary problem. That sounds glib and people nod their heads in agreement without really contemplating the implications of such a rash act. But people who commit suicide out of emotional upset do more damage than most people realize. At the time, a suicidal soul sees it as a rational choice. In fact, in order to go through with this very extreme action, they must see suicide as the only possible alternative to their situation. All they can see is their pain and many feel others will be better off without them. And at this point, Father Thomas felt that he was already dead - spiritually, mentally, and emotionally. His actual physical death would just complete the job. But what the person rarely realizes is that the ramifications of a suicide create a deep and glaring wound in the soul itself.

Brother Thomas was a Catholic clergyman. And suicide is an unforgivable sin in the Roman Catholic view. You would think that the implications for his soul's future incarnations would have stopped him from committing this most mortal of mortal sins. Yet it didn't. Brother Thomas' emotional pain was so great he was able to tell himself that God would understand and forgive him. So, he was able to leave the monastery early one morning before the others woke with a clear plan: to end the pain. He went to a nearby grove of trees within sight of his beloved turret library. Without much ceremony and very little thought, he hung himself with a leather harness he had brought from the monastery's stable.

It can be argued that all human emotional pain is self-inflicted. Our world can be a heaven or a hell depending on our perspective. There were many alternatives Thomas could have employed that would have him live another day, learning and growing from the experience. But this is the one that Thomas chose. There were even ways Thomas could have avoided the problem of the bishop's nephew in the first place. Thomas could have simply asked the young nobleman, "what do you want?" He would have learned that all the young man wanted was to get a diploma from Brother Thomas. The class was just a meaningless formality to the young man. Thomas could have told the reluctant student, *"A young man like you doesn't need this class. You can come if you want. But clearly you have the background and breeding to be a leader in the church."* Thomas could have then happily gone back to teaching. Instead, his desire for self-importance made him miserable enough to eventually end his own life.

In my practice as a hypnotist and coach, I often work with people who are in great emotional upset. I have compassion for them. I understand what it is like to suffer severe distress without seeing a way out. But often I wish I could just snap my fingers and get the client to see there is nothing wrong other than the way he or she is thinking about their situation. And sometimes with hypnosis that is exactly what I am able to do. The result can be transformational. I have seen a sudden, simple realization change lives. I wish somebody had shaken some sense into Brother Thomas before he let this perceived sleight destroy his life with a ripple effect that carried over 500 years later to the life of a young boy born in New York, New York.

Life is not fair.

It does not treat us the way we would like to be treated – not always, at least. But on the spiritual path, if one is paying attention, opportunities are always being presented for growth and transformation. It's a cliché that "there are no problems only opportunities" and rarely does this thought offer much relief to a person trapped in disappointment. But it is nothing less than an axiom in the world of spiritual growth and development, though it rarely seems that way. The "gift of desperation" is not usually received as a welcome gift. It is only after the fact when learning has been incorporated that the true nature of the crisis reveals itself. Brother Thomas never got to that level. He killed himself. The lesson was not learned. It was just deferred.

It would be a misconception to think past-life work always results in an immediate healing. My over-sensitive psyche was not instantly toughened up as I got in touch with Brother Thomas. But I will say I felt a huge and immediate shift. Within several days, the issue that was keeping me up at night lost its power like a balloon with the air let out. I felt inexplicably freed. This is the kind of relief that is available to the past life journeyer whether as a standalone intervention or as an adjunct to psychotherapy.

Maybe, you might think, this healing came from a release of childhood psychic trauma in this life. You might be right. Who am I to say? Or perhaps there really was a 15th century monk who let his life be destroyed to protect his fragile ego. And, frankly, I don't much care. I know that I no longer have to make myself crazy by insisting that everyone like, respect, or love me. And over the distance of five centuries, I thank Brother Thomas for that learning. And perhaps the spirit of that beautiful monk can now truly rest.

The Fragile Friar's Prayer

My life is good
I know who I am
Brother Thomas
duly ordained
deeply pious
a learned man

I study in my
private room
and teach
in class
young clerics
to be men like me
friars engaged
in prayer, meditation
humility

I know who I am
I have no doubt
God is watching
over me
and God will win out

I am content
At peace
Respected
A man of letters
and God
Wise, Learned
True

Then one day
comes The Nephew
I know better
I know what a sin he is
a blasphemy
in my sacred class

There is no room
for the trespass
of such an abomination
in My Sacred Classroom

He does not want to be there
He says
I know he would rather be
in the brothels
or a public house
with women
and bawdy boys
not clerics and students
learning to grow to be
men of God

So I complain.
Wouldn't you?
I tell the Prior
my mentor
my friend

an abomination
an evil has
crept in
ask his counsel
to step in
and make things right
create order
peace again

But I do not know
The patronage of the Archbishop
Is more important to him
than scripture
the holy word of Christ

Called to His Grace's
Palace
Hardly the House of God
Trembling
Such luxury makes no sense to me
"Who do you think you are?"
He bellows from his heights
"How dare you dishonor
My nephew?
How dare you dishonor me?
You are nothing
A maggot
Nothing in the eyes of God
less in those of men.
Go back to
your hovel
out of my sight."

I stumble
Back to cloister
Back to the night

Everything wrong
Can never be right
God has turned
His back on me
utterly alone
Brother Thomas
duly ordained
a foolish lost man

They put me in the kitchen
like a scullery maid
my mind boiling
not really sane
The only recipe for
Relief that comes
Is a rope
and a long walk
to the old oak tree
trusting perhaps God will
Finally have mercy
on me

Yes, I know suicides
are an
abomination against
God
And that is why
if you look
with the eye of
your soul
you may see me still
hanging there:
Brother Thomas
duly ordained
a foolish lost man

Pray for me
a duly ordained
deeply pious
learned man
hanging by his pride
dead by his own hand
hoping God will have
mercy on me

Spirituality can take many forms. The next life I will share with you is of another man of faith who also struggles with ego and pride and falls from grace into disgrace.

ROYAL
HOUSEHOLD
GUARD

(EGYPT – 2000-1000 BCE)

It cannot be said enough that every life has a worldview created in response to an incarnation's society and culture. A past-life voyager must resist any temptation to bring one's current life perspective into these adventures. The way "you" think, act, and feel in a past life may seem absurd. To a field slave in 19th century Georgia, being a "house slave" may seem like a lofty goal. A peasant woman in rural Russia may feel she has no higher aspiration than keeping a clean house, providing good meals, and being obedient to her husband. These are hardly the perspectives of a 21st century African American or today's liberated women. But it is necessary to accept a past-life's reality to learn the lesson that awaits you there.

My experience as a household guard for Egyptian royalty during the great days of ancient Egypt, for example, was one that required me to leave my current perspectives completely behind. When I first met this past life, I found him at work. And his place of work and position were an extreme honor. His job was to stand with his back to the wall in an Egyptian royal household worshiping its members. They were living gods to him. The privilege of being allowed to humbly worship as a household guard was a great honor.

Maybe, like me, you have had the experience of watching the guards at Buckingham Palace. They really do just stand motionless for long periods of time gazing outward. Whatever they think during these vigils is their business. It is private to them. As a guard in a royal household, my thoughts were not supposed to be my own. I had been trained to use these moments of standing meditation for adoration and worship of my employers. I was not expected to just stand at attention: my role was absolute adoration. My appointment to this position exceeded any expectations I might have had for my life. I had arrived. And I wanted nothing more than to continue in this role as long as the gods would allow me. I am sure that I would have been more than happy to spend the remainder of my life in such a wonderful vocation. Perhaps, when the physical demands became too strong, I might have moved on to instruct other young men in this form of service.

When I think back on this life across the millennia that separate us, it seems that I was not a perfect candidate for this work. I imagine a perfect candidate would have been utterly un-distractible. I was not. The royal family had a young child: a toddler or maybe a little older. This young god took a child's interest in me. I wore some kind of tunic with sandals and straps tied up to my calves. The toddler had a habit of pulling at my tunic and sandal straps. He had done this on several occasions. But one afternoon something rattled me. Maybe I was tired. Maybe I allowed my natural adult annoyance at a misbehaving child to surface. I broke the worshipful trance. I became present in my body and moved. I do not think I tried to shoo the boy away, nothing that overt. But my reaction was noticed by one of the family members who made a complaint to my superior. I found myself immediately transferred to a farm working as a farm hand. I had probably already moved into middle age. The farm work would be physically brutal. But, after all, I was still a slave and had some value.

The work was hard and dirty. I think we were raising cotton, but it might have been other crops as well. I lived in a rough rural bunkhouse with other male slaves. I had literally fallen from the heights. I had been in direct, daily contact with living deities. Now I lived and worked with rough men. This was the only life they had ever known. They did not like me. I did not like them. They felt I thought I was superior to them. And they were right. So, they reveled in my disgrace. It gave them pleasure to see the shame and self-disgust that burned within me and made me vulnerable to their taunts and disdain.

I do not think I lived on the farm long. I doubt I could have. Shortly after my fall, I died friendless, hopeless, disgraced.

As I write this narrative, I begin to see common themes emerging. Perhaps the reader will as well. Brother Thomas and now this palace guard? A common theme in which I think that I am better than other people and yet fear I am less than others? Is this my fate? Life after life my ego pulls me into heart-breaking downfalls. I never seem to have had a really secure position in the world. I always seem to be dependent on others for status and feeling like an outsider.

There is that old admonition that those who do not remember the past are condemned to repeat it. This certainly seems to apply to the rule of karma. The karmic question I departed that life with was something like, "why don't people treat me fairly?"

Since then, I have lived out the question, repeatedly. At core, it is a self-centered perspective – looking inward through the imagined eyes of others. It is looking for outside validation for the sense of self-worth and, therefore, a doomed strategy. This I know now and I am happy to report that through this work I am far more interested in what I can contribute to life than what people may think of me. I did not know this millennia ago as a guard intoxicated by my own importance in the pharaoh's palace.

THE LITTLE BOY

Gods They Were
Living Gods
Though
Part of Me
Must have known
they were
just living men,
women,
a child.

Yet how they glowed
magnetic with Power
and Prestige

My teachers told me
to lose myself in
their magnetic majesty
and never let my worship
be tainted by an
inward focused mind.

They must have seen
something in me
I was blind to -
a flaw

Perhaps they knew
I would think
how lucky and favored
I was
to be this close to
the GODS

But when the elders
spoke of
The GODS' Greatness
and said Their Brilliance
Would Be blinding

All I heard
was how great I was
to be chosen to stand
and guard
this close to
perfection

Now I know
The Only God I
truly worshipped
was
the Pharaoh in my
own mind

And for this hubris
I paid a heavy price

The next life I will introduce you to had very little interest in spiritual matters. He was deeply invested in the here and now in a life that gave him comfort, power and prestige. But the issues he faced are central to those I am called on in this life to overcome: feelings of betrayal, mistrust of authority and a karmic moment when a life of success and privilege gets overturned in a moment.

CATTLE RANCHER
FOR THE PHAROAH

(EGYPT – DURING BUILDING OF PYRAMIDS)

I have come to realize that a central theme in my autobiographies is lack of trust – not just trust of authorities, but also of good fortune. I have always loved the John Lennon song "Instant Karma." The idea that one can be going along happy in whatever bubble of security and happiness one finds oneself and then BANG. Everything changes in a moment.

The Day I Will Die Will Be Just Like Any Other Day Only Shorter.

But sudden change does not have to be a physical death. Often, as I go through my exploration of past lives, I experience lives that change utterly in an instant. These sudden upheavals come from forces outside my control, revealing that my trust in something or someone was very misplaced. These are deaths not of a body, but of a way of life. One was a royal guard who loses his position as a result of a single mistake. Another was my life as a successful cattle rancher in ancient Egypt.

In this life, I have the experience of being an unmistakable success. I have people who work for me and many cattle that I own and raise. As I review this life, I find myself working with my animals and my helpers: I also find myself counting my money in my mind.

My major "account" is the royal family and the military. I provide fat, healthy cattle to be slaughtered to feed those in authority and the bellies of those who serve them. It felt secure. I feel fortunate to be in such a good position not to have to worry about things other men have to be concerned about. I know, of course, that the pharaoh was engaged in a great building project: his new pyramid for his final resting. It never occurs to me that not all the people who are building this magnificent monument are volunteers happy for the honor. Some, I discover, have been drafted into service and slavery with relentless hard work, poor rations, and physical abuse. So, imagine my shock and surprise when the pharaoh's men come not only to collect the latest shipment of cattle but also to collect me. I remember my disorientation and confusion. It was an altered state of consciousness. In the modern area, I would liken it to somebody who gets arrested for a white-collar crime and is indignant – the kind who huffily says, "do you know who I am?" I remember pointing out that this must be a mistake. I am a contractor with the pharaoh. I protest as I gradually come to realize that I am to be brought to work on the project – the meat I was to provide would not only be my cattle but in the form of my own body. "This has to be very wrong" I think "some kind of horrific mistake." The men who come do not care what I think. It begins to dawn on me that the people I have been providing my cattle to have betrayed me: I mean nothing to them. I was never really one of them. Doubtlessly, my land and cattle were to be given to somebody else – to one like them.

This fundamental distrust of authorities is something I have carried over to this life. It is no accident that I have been self-employed since I was 34 years old. As soon as I figured out how to stop working for somebody and make a living on my own, I took the leap. I never liked being beholden to an organization; I never trusted an organization to have my best interests at heart. And I have never looked back. I have the idea, apparently for thousands of years, that ultimately you have to look out for yourself.

I am tied, bound, and brought to the construction site. Building a pyramid was literally back breaking, life-crushing work. One of things I like most about past life exploration is noticing things that seem strange and unexpected. My sense was that these stones were roughly as tall, wide, and deep as a man's height.

But of course, they seemed much taller since we were all bent down under the weight. What was unexpected was that we rolled these huge stones on rollers – wooden rollers – and to lubricate the rollers, some of us applied palm leaves for their lubrication. This struck me as logical but only after I "saw" it, wondered what those green things were and then figured it out. Ah, they are leaves for moisture and slipperiness.

The work was just that: moving large, huge stones into position, aside from the engineering part of which I knew nothing. I push. Or I pull. I remember looking behind and seeing the debris. These included bits of wood broken off from the rollers, scatterings of leaves, but also blood staining the ground. I remember at least one of my fellow slave's broken body – human debris discarded behind us where he had simply given up to die. I have a clear sense this was not an unusual occurrence. My life did not continue long after I am taken from my cattle ranch. I have no idea whether I die from overwork, under nourishment and exhaustion, or an accident. But I do remember the lesson from this life very clearly. That lesson is simply that you never know what is going to happen and, if you are going to trust anyone, make sure they are worthy of your trust.

I also got the idea that a life can, and often does, end in a moment. And that does not necessarily mean a physical death. Sometimes it is death of a lifestyle. Sometimes your body lives but your will to live dies. It can be gradual or instant.

But when it happens everything changes. It will happen to me in this life. It will happen to you. It happens to each of us life after life.

I have no doubt that when you, dear reader, review your own "autobiographies" you will discover your own set of themes and life lessons. Those I present here are personal to me. They are presented as examples of the kind of growth and learning that is available to anyone through past life exploration.

And I am happy to say that I have experienced much healing in this life. It has not been a life without its challenges, but I think it has been a time for me of consolidation, healing, and growth. I believe this is why I have been drawn to past life work to incorporate centuries of learning – a life of relative peace to catch my breath and prepare for what is next.

Take my problem with trusting those in authority.

To process it, I chose (or so I believe) to be born as the son of an alcoholic father. You see, there are certain characteristics of those raised by an active alcoholic parent. Children of alcoholics – like children raised in war zones – grow up with prolonged elevated fear. Fear, of course, is a fundamental core emotion felt by every living creature. The flight, fight, or freeze impulse is an essential survival tool. Children of active alcoholics fear that at any moment something bad may happen. This is because from time to time something unexpected and threatening does happen routinely in our alcohol-dominated homes. We learn naturally to be on guard for our own protection against those whom we want most to please and whose care and protection are essential for our very survival. We learn at an early age not to trust those in authority *because they are not trustworthy* even though they are supposed to be. We are forced to deal with the paradox of loving someone we also fear. Gradually, we come to expand this attitude to mistrust anyone in authority not just our parents or guardians. Love and intimacy and being part of any social structure can become difficult for us.

We began to look for signs of untrustworthiness in teachers, coaches, clergy, and anyone else who had power over us. Our capacity for intimacy is reduced. Naturally, hyper-vigilant to the possibility of abuse, we often see it where it is not present and avoid situations that we cannot control in anticipation of betrayal.

When you do past life work, you soon discover that every life has at least one central theme. This seems to be mine – or one of the more prominent – the issue of trust, especially of authorities.

So, you cannot trust the pharaoh, the czar, the government, or even those closest to you, who or what is left? The answer is yourself and perhaps God. Please understand I am not talking about any particular human characterization of God. All religions have their own take on the Creator. And many of them will cheerfully go to war with you if you disagree with their conclusions. But, if you think about it, the belief that a Creator – something outside us – exists is built into the very fabric of human consciousness. It might be the feeling you get when you stand at the shore of a mighty ocean, watch the stars at night, look at the face of your newborn baby after the miracle of birth, or even just listen to a quiet voice inside you that suggests there is more to all this than the day-to-day of your mundane existence.

It may seem like a digression, but I believe it is not. I believe this search for closeness to and alignment with The Creator brings us by an indirect route to trust and connection with others of our kind.

As we choose lives that allow us to develop and refine these themes and work toward perfection, we are able, I believe, to be more and more in partnership with others and God Itself.

So why all the adversity? Why did I not choose to be a successful cattle rancher, supplier of high-quality beef to the Pharaoh, *who lives a long and happy and prosperous life and dies contented in his bed with his loving wife and children by his side instead of one who gets betrayed into a life of misery and enslavement*? Certainly, a life like that would have been easier and far more pleasant. I think the answer is that the Soul I am was up for some growth and chose that life. It chose my parents, society, gender, DNA-driven physical and temperamental characteristics and even the events that unfolded as I join the rest of humanity moving toward what is next for us as a species and as an Overall Soul.

I have heard people describe planet Earth as Spiritual Kindergarten. I hope I have graduated into the first grade or at least am out of pre-school. But I have also concluded that in my case, I am at best a very slow learner.

A Landowner's Lament

I was the king of my own world
Those who toiled raising
My cattle knew it and
knew I could be trusted

Together we provided
Healthy beautiful beasts
for the Pharaoh
The best in the land

Every so often
They come
And I deliver
by contract
paid richly per
animal head

A proud man
with a grateful
heart and mind

But, oh, how it ends
So very unfair
I feel I am one of them
Cattleman, rancher
Lord
of my own domain

Though not noble
yet a man of property
nobility of character
if not of birth

They come to my land
they drink my wine
we laugh together
tell stories
until late evening time

I am comfortable
with their company
Important on my own land
a master of property
owner of men

Then one day
they come as if
in a rage for some
unknown sleight
something I had
not done

They come not to trade and deal
in an honest way
they come to take
giving nothing
in return
only pain – so much pain

I realize
I have been
a deluded man
in fact a Fool
They say that I am nothing
just something to be taken
and used

They take my cattle
my freedom
my pride
They take me to work on their monument
the Pharaoh's glory
His afterlife tomb

They say there is honor in it
building a tomb for a living God
but for those who move the giant stones
with our legs and back
there is simply blood, sweat
the pain of pushing
and being pushed

They said to think of the Glory
of what we are building:
A home for an ever-lasting Deity
not what has been destroyed

If I had this life to do over
I would be a completely different man
not a grateful eager servant
but a confident independent man

I would treat my slaves differently
and see them as men
not just for what they could do for me

My land was beautiful
fertile and rich
the gods so smiled upon me
I forgot I was born a little man
in a big world run by power,
privilege and greed

where words of the Powerful
to one such as me
mean nothing
hieroglyphic fantasies etched
onto another man's shifting sand

Imagine for a minute what it would be like to be transported into the body of a different gender. The next life I will share with you was the first time this happened to me and, if you engage in past life explorations, perhaps will happen to you.

UNA

(MIDEAST – ANCIENT TIMES)

I first met a man who I consider a major influence in my understanding of what is possible through past life exploration – David Quigley – at a hypnotist convention in the summer of 2019. I found David's comfort with his own past life journeys inspiring. My explorations up until that point were always more or less random. The initial past life regression therapy work I did would start with my current emotional state as a jumping off point. The facilitator would then guide the session based on whatever came up in response to the spirit's promptings. Most of my early past life journeys therefore had to do with shedding light on my personality and the challenges I am dealing with in my current life. Quigley had a different take on what is possible in past life exploration. There were maybe 20 of us professional hypnotists in the room. Most of us had had some experience working with past lives both for our own development and helping clients achieve their goals. But I think Quigley's approach struck many of us as both novel and yet – when you think about it – obvious. Quigley suggested that we have the ability through past life exploration not only to surface the deeper causes behind our current life's issues, but also to retrieve skills and abilities we may have had in other lives and bring them back into the present. For example, David spoke convincingly about his own experience tapping into past life skills as a piano player to bring piano playing – musical skills – into his present life. He described how he had been a piano player or harpsichordist in his former incarnations. Sometimes the skills were mediocre, but he found one where the skills were outstanding. He told us that he brought those skills into his current life with great success. He presented the idea that once you identified a life with the skill that you want in your current incarnation, you could simply negotiate with it and incorporate its skills into your current life. He says in this way he very rapidly "learned" to play the piano quite expertly. Learned, in this sense, is a bit of a misnomer. As he described it, it was more like he remembered it.

For those readers who find this extraordinary, ask yourself is this not at least a *possible explanation* for the irrefutable fact that some people do seem to be born knowing things. That elusive human faculty called talent must come from somewhere. Why not a past life?

In our culture (Western European thinking) we have no suitable explanation for this phenomenon. But when the Tibetans search for a new ruler and spiritual leader, their impulse is to search for the reincarnation of the Dalai Lama. When they find a young boy who seems to know certain things – who identifies objects owned or dear to the former Dalai Lama – they decide this is the one. He becomes the next Dalai Lama. Here you have an entire culture willing to accept the simple principle that soul memory survives death and can indeed be reborn in subsequent incarnations. Ian Stevenson's *Twenty Cases Suggestive of Reincarnation* offers credible documentation of children born with verifiable past life recollections. It is worth a read before discarding this possibility – or any of the ideas presented here – without serious consideration.

So, when Quigley asked us what quality we would like to bring into our current life, I chose the quality of leadership. I assumed it would be useful in my work and chose this quality without thinking much about it other than no one can have too much leadership ability. Upon reflection, I realize that my notion of leadership came from a distinctly male perspective. A leader I pictured as someone who is strong, decisive, and certainly a little bossy. And, of course, I assumed a leader had the quality of vision and the ability to inspire others to follow him.

Our facilitator guides us into trance, and we begin our journeys.

Almost immediately I find myself in ancient times in the Mideast: Alexandria. I encounter myself, however, in a way I had never experienced life before. I experience myself as a woman. I think her name was Una. She is in a boat with rowers and some sails moving toward the dock of an ancient city. I clearly remember the construction of the city. That is what stuck in my mind; it was my first impression, the way the buildings were made and my intense interest in them. They were stone or baked clay forms and sun hardened. I attend to the details of their construction with a knowledgeable eye. The boat lands at a dock. I realize I am here to meet my sons. I also sense that my boys are the single most important part of my life. How does this experience relate to leadership? At first, I am confused by that and simply enjoy the novel experience of being a middle-aged woman in ancient Alexandria. Then I begin to realize that my sons are highly successful in the construction trade. They are known far and wide as builders of large public buildings and grand homes. I am their coach and mentor. My children are extensions of me. They are a part of me. And they seek my counsel on everything they do even though now grown with families of their own. My boys value their mother's advice. They seek it out and I give it gladly.

Yet to the world my sons are the authors of their success – strong and independent. No one knows I am the mover and visionary behind the scenes. No one sees my steady hand. There once was a husband, but he is long gone, barely a memory. The boys are mine – of me and belonging to me.

When I met Una, she is no longer young. I have the sense that for many years she has guided her boys toward success, personally and in business. Her model of leadership is a feminine one – maternal – she is their muse and support.

How do you know a past life experience is more than simply telling yourself a story? One way to me is when I experience and feel things in a way that is completely unfamiliar and surprising. In my current life, I am a father and grandfather. I had no idea that being a mother is so completely different. Una's boys were big men physically as well as in society. I revel in their stature. I feel they are part of me. They came from my body and, though they are separate and living in the world, they belong to me absolutely. Possession, not as manipulation, just a simple emotion. They are mine. I love them without reservation.

A man may understand that children come from a woman's body – were indeed once a part of her body – and therefore, a woman might have a different perspective about parenthood from that of a man. But as I meet Una, I FEEL it, suddenly and vividly. In Robert Heinlein's book *Stranger in A Strange Land*, he called this deep knowing "grokking" – a way of knowing beyond simple understanding of the fact. So, at the risk of being glib, I can say that I feel that I now deeply can appreciate what it is like to be a mother in a way that never would have been available to me without this experience.

And Una was an extraordinary mother. I knew her boys genuinely loved and respected her. They wanted what she wanted. She is coach, teacher, and cheerleader. This is not to say Una was not tough. She was. Una could be sharp with her comments. But her shrewdness and toughness were tempered with love and a genuine desire for them to be all they can be.

Yet, as I have often reminded you, nobody gets through a lifetime without tragedy. Una was no exception. When directed to move forward to a significant time in that life, I found myself overwhelmed with emotion as I learn that my youngest son died in a construction accident. My grief is total. My life is never the same from that point on. When I have three sons, my life feels centered, successful, and secure. With three pillars, I am steady, and life make sense. With one of them gone, I feel horribly unbalanced.

Una is never happy again after her youngest child's death. From that point on, she is a broken woman. She simply goes through the motions of life until her death.

David Quigley asked us to consult with the life we had uncovered and ask it in the world of spirit if it would be willing to bring its talents into our own current incarnation. In this way, we would bring part of ourselves from the past that is useful to our current situation. My incarnation as Una agreed she would come into my life as my coach and mentor if I would agree to act in place of the third of her sons. A win-win contract.

Has my life changed significantly since this encounter? I am not sure. And I believe any change from past life work is usually subtle, but what I do know is I have an appreciation of women and motherhood that I had never had before. I now better understand my wife's terrible anxiety when she feels any of them are not doing as well as she would like in life.

In terms of leadership, I have learned to push my ego out of the way in my work as a coach and mentor. More than ever, my work with people is all about them and their success and I feel myself more and more as a channel for healing, not its source.

A MOTHER'S FOUNDATION

I built my family
and my family built a world.
It was such a site to see

Anywhere in Alexandria
Royal buildings
Palaces
Public Buildings by the Sea
Monuments to my three
Beautiful boys
Towering men
Builders all
From my own tiny womb
Part of my flesh
A mother's pride

Three pillars standing strong

Big Men
Proud Men
Strong Men

To whom no challenge
is too big
Armies of artisans
And laborers bow
At their feet
Princes and Potentates
Court them
Alexandria's
Great Builder Brothers

And they honor me
Let me guide them
Accept my counsel

They come to me with questions
mama this?
Mother that?
Should I do this?
Should I do that?

I always say
if it were me, I would do this.
If it were me, I would not do that.
Sometimes I say
beware of this one
he is too sly
Or get close to that one
avoid this one
he has an evil heart
or dark soul
flatter this one
he can do you great good

My boys' women are gentle
Loving and true
Obedient to my sons

as my boys are good
and obedient with me

Then one horrible day
the Gods turn against me
One dark moment the light
of my life went out
never to return.
My baby died.
The littlest one
so gentle and fair

I wish I could say
he died in his mother's arms
with a mother's love
comforting him
but no
he fell far away

I heard this one fateful day
His servant comes and speaks
such awful words
"your son is dead"
That is how he said it
"your son is dead"

How do you say that to a mother?
I had him beat
For being so ill-mannered
And cast into the street

That servant ripped out my heart
that day
And he had not even bothered to wash his feet

He killed all that was good that day
His words broke my soul

And it is broken still
How could it not?

Infants die
That we women understand
But a big strong powerful man
To join the Gods

No mother is meant
To lose a son like that

People say "look at your other boys
you have much to live for"
but all I can see is sorrow

A mother lives to love and guide
Her sons
These towering, big men from my
womb grew to build a city

I built a strong foundation.
Three beautiful sons
I gave to the world
When one was taken
My World was taken from me.
There is no reason to go on.

Their constructions now torment
my heart and eyes
grotesque monuments
to a mother's broken heart.

Another principle of past life exploration is the importance to being open to literally whatever you experience without judgement. Once I spend the better part of an hour reliving a past life as an insect. I know some people who write about past lives say this doesn't happen – that we always incarnate as people – but I settled back and enjoyed the sight of blades of grass looking like trees and was amazed at how the surface tension in a drop of water holds it as a dome of fluid from the perspective of an insect crawling around it. And you must be also prepared for some lives to be the exact opposite of the way you are in this one. The next life I will share with you was one of those.

ZEKE

(USA SOUTHWEST – EARLY 19th CENTURY)

I enjoy watching crime shows like *Law and Order*. I like them because, in a single episode, the bad guy is usually caught and punished. It is gratifying to feel that life is fair and justice will always prevail.

Rarely does real life play out this way.

In real life, most often the rich generally get richer; the poor usually get poorer. In the real world, people do horrendous crimes, yet seem to prosper. Those cases when real life justice works like on television are few and far between. Occasionally, a famous TV evangelist preaches family values. Then he gets caught soliciting a transvestite prostitute and is publicly shamed. But more often they get away with it. Or they buy their way out of the problem with secret non-disclosure agreements. Sometimes a mob boss is betrayed by his lieutenant and goes to jail for his crimes. Mostly they fade into benign obscurity. Their descendants become respected pillars of the community within a generation or two. Karma is far more subtle and patient than these examples.

"What goes around" does not usually "come around" like some cosmic boomerang. It may seem unfair that bad acts go unpunished. But that is the way here. Karma just waits patiently to be worked out in the next life or the ones after that.

My life as the son of a wealthy rancher in early 19th century America was as close to a kind of instant karma as you usually get. The price he paid for his crime, though not in kind, was relatively immediate. Crime and punishment seemed to be played out in a single lifetime.

I became aware of him in a past-life therapist's pleasant office one bright spring day. I am not sure what his name was: it may have been Zeke or Zac. I do not think it matters. And by the end of his life, I doubt even he remembered it or cared that he had forgotten. So, let us call him Zeke.

Let me introduce him to you.

First, you need to know Zeke was not particularly bright. He was certainly illiterate. No one would have called him a thoughtful boy or man. But he was shrewd. He was shrewd enough to realize that as the son of a wealthy rancher he could do things less privileged boys and men could not. In fact, he discovered early on that he could get away with most anything without negative consequences. I do not believe Zeke's mother was around for much of his life and his father was relatively disinterested in the kind of man his son was becoming. He may even have shared young Zeke's "I am above the law of God and Man" attitude himself. So, Zeke ran wild.

He was also by nature a loner; he did not have lot of friends nor did he feel that was a deprivation. The isolation of a cattle ranch in the early 1800s was a contributing factor, but more likely it was simply the way Zeke was wired. He was completely focused on Zeke – what Zeke needed and wanted was all that mattered.

Zeke liked girls and he liked having sex with girls whether the girls liked it or not. He discovered in his teenage years that he could force himself on servant girls in neighboring ranches. And nothing would happen to Zeke, which was all that mattered. It is true that on at least one occasion he pushed his romantic attentions with violence. He hit a servant girl in an isolated barn and broke her jaw. But he was not moved by her tears or pleas for mercy. With callous disregard for what he had done, he explained that nobody would believe her. He would say that she had lured him into the barn and blame the victim for his crime. Who would doubt him? He was after all the son of a respected property owner. And Zeke was right. Nothing happened. Just a pleasant memory he would return to for solitary pleasurable recollection, committing the crime over and over in his lust-clouded mind.

When I first encountered Zeke, I had the impression that rape is something he may have done many times and without consequences. These experiences reinforced Zeke's belief that he could do anything he wanted with women or girls provided no one was looking and his victims were not important people.

All this changed one fateful day. Zeke was out riding his horse and came upon a stream where an attractive young neighbor girl was resting alone. He saw this as an invitation to do what he wanted. It can be argued that inside many males beats the heart of a rapist; the line between manly assertiveness and rape can seem blurry to some men and Zeke was certainly one of these. But the only thing consensual about this encounter was that Zeke gave himself permission to do whatever he wanted.

Zeke's whole world view was Zeke-centric. He wanted what he wanted when he wanted it. And, as I mentioned, he was not intellectually gifted; yet Zeke was shrewd. He identified this girl resting by the stream as not somebody who was from an important family and therefore, fair game. He jumps her and has his way with her. Zeke is strong from farm work and youth. She is young, female, and does not have the ability to resist him. But, unlike the girl in the barn who was timid and felt powerless to get justice, this new target has fire in her eyes and in her heart. She is outraged and is not about to let this go as an unfortunate incident that occurred to her one lazy summer afternoon. She is not the type to "forgive and forget" or worse still blame herself for being alone and unprotected and therefore culpable. She fights him with every fiber of her being. But her efforts are not enough to save her from Zeke's ravaging. Spent from his exertions, Zeke steps back and she hisses at him with fists clenched and says "I am going to tell my brothers and they are going to get you for this. You are a dead man."

Was her defiant nature something Zeke had not considered? Or was he under the impression she did not know him and what ranch he was from? Or was he simply blinded by lust that day? Or was it all of the above? But this was not what Zeke was expecting. He panics. There is a struggle. She resists further. And Zeke hits her powerfully on the face. She falls and hits her head on a large stone. She is dead.

Zeke panics.

One of the characteristics of past life exploration is that the past life voyager experiences emotions that occurred during the past life. In Zeke's case, in this moment, his entire body vibrated with upset and his mind went into a confused blank. Fight, flight or freeze? Zeke chose flight. It was a visceral reaction to the sight of her lifeless body.

It never occurs to him to do something clever – to try to hide the body and cover his tracks. There were not even any witnesses. Perhaps, he could have gotten away with it. Maybe no one would ever connect him with the young female corpse by the stream. There were certainly other ways for Zeke to handle this problem than the way he chose. But the only way that occurred to Zeke was to return to his ranch, pack some supplies, and run away.

Again, it is important to know, that Zeke was not especially bright. Zeke's idea of running away to safety was to go to the next county and hide out. For the rest of his life, Zeke remained in hiding. He had only fled to the next county and was terrified that people would recognize him. He feared he would be held accountable as a murderer and rapist, not only spending years in jail but also bringing shame to his father. He never returned to his home and became a recluse. Zeke had some basic skills, and he was able to survive by hunting and working odd jobs. He became known as the hermit of the hills, a local legend. His hair grew long. His beard obscured his features. He avoided people except when necessary to secure occasional odd jobs.

Sometimes a life ends peacefully surrounded by loved ones after a life of accomplishment and service. Other lives end unexpectedly and violent. Zeke's end came about as a result of canned meat – or so at least that is what Zeke believed. Food poisoning.

Around this time, people were traveling through the west on their way to California. It was a long trip along the way wagons often needed repair. And Zeke had these skills from his early years on his father's cattle ranch. One extremely hot summer day, Zeke was working on a settler's wagon doing odd repair jobs. The family paid this peculiar, bearded man for his labor with canned foods they had brought from Ohio on their journey. Canned foods were relatively new on the scene and these were tin. The science of canning was not exact, so food poisoning was not unknown. As Zeke, alone in his camp among the rocks and hills, lay in agony, he was convinced that the canned food was killing him. He may have been right. It is impossible to tell. But he did die alone and in great discomfort.

Karma, as they say, can be a bitch. As Zeke lay dying, he had a moment of hope. Into his camp came a couple of young men on horses and they stumbled upon Zeke and his simple campsite. Zeke allowed himself some hope that these young men might rescue him. What they did was laugh and take Zeke's mule and saddle plus anything else they found that might be of use in his humble camp. What I remember most is they even took the coarse wool blanket that was keeping Zeke's shivers at bay and laughed as they rode away.

So ends the very sad, lonely life of Zeke the rancher's son.

I genuinely feel that the karma of the bad action against the woman Zeke raped was paid back in that lifetime. He did his penance within that life. I am not sure whether he connected it directly and felt remorse. But none the less, he paid the price. One carryover from his life that perhaps I brought into mine was Zeke's mistrust of people. Initially, Zeke had to stay distant from people to protect his identity and avoid being brought to justice for the crime of rape and murder. But this distancing and mistrust of people became a lifestyle. Zeke was absolutely alone in life.

How much of that feeling of isolation, if any, I brought into this life is something that I ponder.

Another possible karmic echo of Zeke is a natural chivalry I have always had believing that women are deserving of respect. An appropriate emotion I am sure you will agree for a self-admitted former 19th century rapist.

Fugitive

I got away with it
I really did
they never caught me
now they never will

I did not want to kill her
I did not want to do a crime
I wanted just to touch her
just felt like having a good time

But she said she had brothers
guess I should have known
pushed her
she fell
I had to run
the life of a fugitive to be mine

I did not need to run too far
to be safe – just far enough

The hills are a good place
where a man can run and hide
change his name
hide his crime

The schoolteacher lady said
a rose by any other name
should smell as sweet
my name long have I forgotten

My crime lives in my mind
sometimes I wonder if it
can be seen by those I pass by
the man I was beneath
the hideous thing I have become

Longhaired
crazy eyes
filthy rags
the furtive glance
a fugitive needs to survive

I will mend your pots
grease your axles
shoe your horses
I can do a little
or a lot
provided you are only passing
through or like me
a forgotten soul who
has learned
not to see

The hills are a world
where a man can lose himself
so I did find
until I forgot what I was running from
and simply ran
a lonesome, sad
forgotten, empty man

I remember to never show
my true face to woman or man
So, if you pass by
look through or around me
do not mark my eyes
an invisible man

If you want to find me
Look for the fugitive
in the hills
where if you dig deeply
I may finally let you
find me
Buried beneath
a boulder
of guilt, fear
and shame
in a self-dug
anonymous grave

Usually, the issues that we face in this life can be traced back to some childhood trauma or breach of trust and I would never suggest that past-life work is the first place to look for causes to emotional or behavioral problems. But when all else fails, you may find the answer you are looking for not in this life but in a prior incarnation. Whether it is a true karmic issue or not may become irrelevant provided the healing takes place.

I found the next lives I will share with you are in response to the question, "why did I develop a problem with substance abuse in my current incarnation?"

PROBLEMS
WITH ALCOHOL

(LOCATIONS UNKNOWN – STONE AGE AND
EUROPE MIDDLE AGES)

As a child of a self-admitted alcoholic, I grew up with certain insecurities. I now know these insecurities are typical of children of alcoholics. In my house there was always the fear of the unexpected. What kind of mood would dad be in? Happy-go-lucky Dad or the Father from Hell?

I do not want to overstate how bad it was at home. Others have had far worse situations. Many grew out of these rough starts in life to become healthy, successful adults. Of course, many do not. And all bear some emotional scars whether crippling or just an underlying feeling of things being not quite right. Maybe I was by nature a more sensitive child than most. My parents used to say I was "high strung" or "over-sensitive." These might have been appropriate descriptions, but these descriptions also took on a life of their own. I came to see myself as less than other children. Less competent. Less valuable. I was uncomfortable in social settings and still can be to a degree. But when I had just turned 16, some neighborhood girls invited me to my first high school dance. They knocked at my front door and almost dragged me there. I will always be grateful for that intervention. At that dance, I discovered a magic elixir that night: a quart bottle of Miller beer.

You can imagine a skinny, incredibly nervous young man walking into that dance. The music was amazing. Hardcore early 60s rock and roll. I was terrified but had never felt so completely alive. This was life and action. This was the big time and, though I felt on the outside looking in, I wanted in. I longed to be part of it all.

I had my eye on a certain girl. She was a friend. I wrote poetry and short stories simply for the pleasure of showing them to her and getting a little of her attention. There she was, looking sexy and incredible. And she had her arms draped around some guy. Her boyfriend, I discovered that night. I was devastated. The world I wanted to be part of looked unattainable. I felt small and alone.

Then a friend suggested we leave the dance and go out drinking. I had never drunk alcohol in my life. I had a strong aversion to alcohol as a result of my father's drinking. After all, alcohol was the root of many of the problems in my home. Nonetheless, I felt I had to get away from watching the girl of my dreams making out with her boyfriend. So, I left. It turned out there was a neighborhood convenience store that would sell beer to anybody who had the cash. We went to an empty lot next to the store and I drank my first beer. It was love at first taste. I doubt I really became intoxicated that night. But the idea of being drunk itself gave me cover to be free. I left the dance a shy, bookish kid. I returned as "cool kid." It was an immediate transformation. It wasn't that I found myself that night. I found a way to be who I wanted to be. I went back into the dance and danced. I had discovered the answer to the problem of being me. And I was to follow that path for the next 18 years with great enthusiasm.

My coming of age happened to coincide with the era of sex and drugs and rock n' roll. All my heroes were drug users and heavy drinkers. Rolling Stones. The Beatles. Jack Kerouac. Allen Ginsberg. The list goes on and on and nary a teetotaler amongst them. I became what is known as a functional alcoholic and drug user. I graduated college in the top 10% of my class for my undergraduate degree and went on to graduate school. I had a successful career in advertising. I married a beautiful, intelligent woman. We had children, purchased homes. But the desire to escape was always within me. And that desire was satisfied by alcohol and drugs. I have a strong motivation if not to succeed at least not to fail. I would shake off the night before and get to work the next day. Like many of my breed, I would put on a front until eventually I got wise to the situation and became sober at around age 34.

It is true that a family history of addiction and a rough childhood would easily explain why I felt so drawn to the relief found in chemical euphoria. But I have also found another possible root cause through the exploration of past lives.

I was at a training program in reincarnation regression hypnosis when the instructor posed a question: "would you be interested in exploring whether a past life might be influencing your current life situation?"

I was.

At the time, I had been happily in recovery from alcohol and substance abuse for decades. I always assumed that my tendency to seek escape from reality was explained by combination of my genetics, upbringing, and maybe some unfortunate decisions. But the thought that a karmic cause might be at play intrigued me. I volunteered to be a test subject.

Almost immediately I found myself on a hunt in what historians would call the stone age.

We are a small hunting group. We are dirty. We smell rank but no one notices. It is just our scent. We have our scent. The animals we hunt have theirs. We do not speak among ourselves. We are focused and patient. We are also hungry and approaching desperation. Our weapons are spears, roughhewn. They are part of us. And we are part of each other: a team or a pack. I think there are four of us. I am neither the oldest or the youngest. I am not the best hunter. Nor am I a straggler. Like the others, I am tired and beginning to feel the breath of hunger for myself and our tribe breathing down my back.

Finally, we manage to disable a large mammal, some kind of boar. It is now the desperate one. It falls on its back, thrashing wild. One of us works his way toward the head to slit its throat and start the blood flow. I am behind the beast's rump when suddenly it kicks me with fury – a hoof flies hard into my groin. I cannot describe the pain. There are no words for such sudden and all-consuming pain.

My companions eventually slit the prey's throat and capture his precious blood. They open the animal's cavity and remove organs. I am on the ground in agony but silent. Eventually, they become aware my condition. They gather around. Their faces are sad. They know this means my end. Yet they stay with me for the rest of the day. They are my friends. We have been on many hunts together. We all know this will be my last. I am in such agony, unspeakable agony. And we all understand what must happen next. They are sad, but stoic. They will carry the food back to the village and leave me to die alone. I expect nothing more.

I watch them tie the animal to a large branch, preparing to bring the sorely needed fresh meat back to the village. Usually, there would be laughter and celebration among us. Now there is only silent resignation. Love and mutual respect have bound us. Before they leave, they bring me a bladder – taken from the animal they have just slaughtered. It is filled with the animal's blood. My heart warms at the kindness. This is all they have to offer me. We know that blood is nourishing. Perhaps they are hoping I will recover. Likely they are merely being kind. The animal has provided plenty of food to fill the village's need. It is not a sacrifice to give a blood to a wounded comrade. They wish me well with nods and touches. Then silently head off on their journey leaving me alone.

It takes several days of constant agony before I die. The pain is absolute and unrelenting. I want so much for oblivion. I want so much for it to end. When I finally do leave my body, I feel my consciousness rising over the scene above trees.

I know when some people recall "passing over" they report that they meet spirit guides and rejoin a spiritual family. There was no sense of that here – just relief and escape. But I did remember very clearly thinking *I never, ever want to experience this pain again. I vow never to experience this kind of pain again.*

The facilitator very wisely says that while this experience was certainly traumatic, it does not seem like the kind of incident that would lead to a pattern of alcoholism and addiction. I am guided to go deeper into trance. I am guided into another life and get my answer.

In this deeper state of trance, I walk through a field of mist to another life. Another body. Another mind.

I find myself in a stone prison cell.

Medieval Europe, I am sure. I know I am European. I am a man – husky and dark. And I have been condemned as a murderer. It happened last night. I was in a tavern. There was an insane drunken argument. I am a big man, enormously powerful. A brute and proud of my strength especially when drunk. I hit somebody too hard. Much too hard. So hard that he dies. They drag me away. I awake still drunk in this prison place. This morning I was judged by a local Lord who condemns me with disdain to death by hanging. A disgraceful way to leave this world. They are organizing the equipment now. I am hungover. Head bursting. Stomach churning. Dry mouth. And so afraid. Despite my manliness and fierce spirit, I am afraid. I have been a violent man. A bully. And now I am about to be hung without pity like a dog. I feel sorry for myself as I dwell on my fate.

I have seen such executions before. I have found them entertaining as I watched the condemned man brought to the scaffold and then dropped. I have slapped my thigh with merriment as his tongue protruded from the mouth and at the gasping, gurgling sounds as the rope squeezes his life from him. I have joked as the smell of his feces and the stain of his piss came into my senses. All part of the spectacle. All part of the day's entertainment. That I am to meet the same public fate terrifies and revolts me. That there is nothing I can do about it – that I am powerless and trapped – maddens me.

Then a miracle happens.

I have a friend. He works in the tower. No one cares or knows about our connection. He brings me, of all things, an animal bladder filled with remarkably strong fortified wine. I am grateful. I drink the wine and become gloriously drunk. The thought crosses my mind that I am cheating the hangman.

As I recall this life, I am lying on the floor in a past life hypnotist's office and laughing a deep throated manly laugh. I got one over on them. The combination of alcohol from the night before and this powerful wine puts me in a place where I could care less what was going to happen. My laughter on the floor in 2019 cold sober does not sound like me. It is deep and full throated.

And I am gloriously, wonderful intoxicated without a drop of mind-altering beverage other than a Starbucks coffee.

I realize that I found a solution to handle any kind of pain in that prison cell: get drunk and escape. Cheat the hangman.

These two lives were vastly different in circumstances. The personalities have nothing in common. But what they share is a common solution to any discomfort. As a stone age hunter gorged by the desperate kick of a wild boar, **I decide I will never suffer this kind of pain again**. As a medieval rogue sentenced to death, I find a solution to the problem of pain. That solution was The Magic Elixir: Alcohol.

In later incarnations, I expanded this solution to apply to any kind of pain including emotional upset. The Beatles song "Day Tripper" had a chorus I took as a metaphor for this chemical solution. They were singing about a lover's frustration over a girl who was in and out of a relationship. She was the "Day Tripper." She left her boyfriend feeling sad, broken hearted. The solution offered was "the easy way out." The fab four sing, "got a good reason for taking the easy way out." And to an addict, a ***good reason*** eventually becomes any reason. After a while, reality itself becomes too uncomfortable to face without a little chemical alteration. Alcohol and drugs are escapes that apparently, I have been dealing with in various forms for tens of thousands of years. A bladder of blood on a hunting trip did not solve the problem of pain. But fill that bladder with strong, fortified wine in a dungeon awaiting execution and I could laugh staring defiantly into the hangman's face.

Now, as fascinating as these two lives were for me to re-experience, they were not characteristic of the themes that I have uncovered in my journey. Usually when I journey to the other side, I bump into issues of self-esteem. I return over and over to struggle with my place in society, my need to be important, listened to, and the center of attention. These two incarnations are simply about pain and a solution – a way out.

As I said, I was 16 when I picked up my first drink. I get invited to my first high school dance by two neighborhood girls. I arrived prepared to be miserable. Then came rescue. I fell in love with the feeling of intoxication and the beverage that delivered it. An alcoholic was born that night.

Was it my destiny to overindulge in booze and eventually drugs?

Maybe. Stone age hunter in horrible pain. Medieval murderer released from fear of impending execution by a bladder full of booze. Or maybe just my genetics and post trauma anxiety caused by being raised in an unstable home. But the solution was undeniable. I was a 16-year-old enjoying life. A teenage drunk on a dance floor intoxicated by youth and life and beer. The only question I had about all this was when can I do it again? However, despite the good times with substances (and there were many), there is always a dark side to this escape mechanism. This pattern – escaping pain and negative emotions through chemicals – became a lifestyle that operated in the background of my life in this life for many years. It short-circuited my development until eventually I became aware that "better living through chemistry" was delivering more pain than pleasure. Then just as suddenly, I was able to stop. This was many years ago and I am grateful for every day of sobriety that has followed.

I consider myself fortunate to have escaped this trap relatively early and easily.

Choosing unconsciousness in this spiritual kindergarten is not a good strategy for spiritual growth. It would be like not doing homework or paying attention at lessons and hoping to graduate at the top of your class. That is just not the way it works. You find yourself sitting in the corner wearing a dunce cap and eventually get left behind to repeat the class until you get it right.

A Drunkard's Way

Oh, it hurts
Hurts so bad
I want to die
Cannot think
Blind red

I know they
are sad for me
See it in their
faces
But all I want is death
sweet death
It takes forever
Days and days until
Finally I float up and above
through the trees
No longer fearing
the beasts that
wait to take what
is left of me

I float into the sky
and declare
with all my soul
NEVER AGAIN

A dying prayer
A decision
A mission

Now in another body
Big and mean
I am the kind of man
who would scare the hell
out of you
in a dark alley
or public bar
Beat you senseless
without fear
You would feel terror and
Give me the respect I demand
for I am THE MAN
Drunk or sober
I could tear a grown man
limb from quivering limb
and smile into his
dying eyes.

But now they want me dead
The Hangman
wants to strangle me
slowly into death
and I am frightened
as I have frightened others

Because I have seen
the bulging orbs
of the poor buggers
helpless in the gallows' square
as the noose tightens life
from flesh held helpless
pissing, shitting while
idlers laugh and jeer
And now that is to be me

A drunkard with hangover
trembling
Terrified with blind raging fear

Then a miracle
Answer to a drunkard's prayer

A goaler – friend -
Big Red The Goaler Man
We have
shared confidences
and brawled
over many a pot of ale
An ally – a friend -
on the day of my death
He does not like the lord
likes his good drinking buddy
much more
and brings me not
a bladder of blood
but something
so much better

A bladder filled
with good strong
blood red wine

And I laugh
Oh how I laugh
Clutch it like
a drowning
man a rescue rope
and drink it down
drunk as a Lord
fooling the Hangman

Fooling the crowd
I go out singing
She's a Good Old Girl
She's a Good old Gal
Roll her over and let me in
laughing and spitting
in the Hangman's
stupid face
and leave this earth
happy that I found
a way
a way up and out
Take me Bacchus
My one true friend
My salvation
Today
Tonight
Forever
Amen

The next life I will share for you was probably the saddest I have yet met though my past life explorations are ongoing and who knows if I might find something to eclipse the sad life of a poor slave boy in Georgia long before the American civil war.

ROBBIE

(USA GEORGIA – BEFORE CIVIL WAR)

Do we choose our parents? Our era and place in the world? Our bodies? Our fate? Past life explorers will affirm without hesitation that we most definitely do. Though it may seem unlikely when so many lives are short and brutal or consist of degradation, terror, and pain. Those of us who have undertaken this exploration generally believe that we choose it all before each birth: the good, the bad, the beautiful, and even the horrific.

It was probably the writings of Louise Hay that first introduced me to the idea that we choose our lives. Along the way, I adopted the commonly accepted notion that Earth is a kind of spiritual kindergarten or perhaps for the more advanced among us, an institute of higher education. I gradually came to believe that each life we choose gives us an opportunity to work on an issue central to our soul's mission. Perhaps you find this a comforting philosophy. The idea of choice makes the idea of those lives that are filled with tragedy more palatable. These include lives that end in infancy, those that seem defined by a crippling handicap, or those that end in a Nazi gas chamber. It might explain why my soul seems to have chosen the life of Robbie, a little black boy born into a life of slavery and abuse in antebellum Georgia. There was little joy in Robbie's life and very much pain. The emotional highlight of his life experience was a "relationship" with another slave named Daisy. And

I think Daisy did little more than show Robbie a moment of kindness that stood out because it was virtually the only time the little "colored boy" knew anything like love in his too long life.

When I first experienced Robbie, it was a shock and far from pleasant. Like many of the incarnations that I seem to have chosen, my experience as Robbie was one of low self-esteem combined with ambition for something better. But in Robbie's case, there was no pretense – no white silk shirt like the officers – just pain and hopelessness. He knew and completely accepted that there was no hope of significant improvement in his circumstances. The future looked to Robbie like more of the past only increasingly worse as he suffered his way into old age.

Robbie was a funny looking little boy. His appearance and awkwardness would cause some people on the plantation where he was born to automatically smile. He was, to put it simply, a comic sight. Big ears. Eyes too far apart. Odd chin. And, as an African-American according to the United States Constitution of the era, Robbie counted for a mere 3/5 of a human being no matter how attractive, intelligent, or accomplished he might be. He was a slave. Chattel. He had no formal rights. He did not have the right to own property or choose where to live. He did not have the right to select his career or get paid for his work. He could not travel. He could not marry. And Robbie knew he could be sold for necessity or at a master's whim. Education was denied to him. Indeed, it was illegal to teach a black child to read in Georgia until long after the civil war. His very survival lay in his master's hands. This is the world Robbie was born into. To compound these obvious painful limitations, Robbie was frail and odd looking. With his ears stuck out and eyes set too far apart, the overall effect was not so much ugly as comic. He was, as a potential buyer was to put it, "a funny looking little creature."

Robbie's greatest ambition was to be what he called a "house slave." He accepted the injustices that defined his life as a matter of course. It was just the way things were.

Families in the slave huts had no protection other than their monetary value as property and a master's goodwill. There was no guarantee that a family would stay together. A slave "marriage" had no legal standing. A "husband" or "wife" could be carried off at a moment's notice. A mother could be sold off separate from her child. And this is what happened to Robbie when his mother is sold at auction and he simply became emotionally and physically alone in the world.

When a past life traveler connects with a prior incarnation, it always starts with a particular experience. Usually, but not always, these are significant moments in the incarnation story. The facilitator asks questions like: "Are you male or female? Are you indoors or outdoors? How old do you feel you are? What is going on? And how do you feel emotionally?" When I connected with Robbie, I am outdoors at a slave auction. I am being put up for sale. And the sale is not going well. The potential buyer does not really want me. Not at any price. Too scrawny for a field hand. Too stupid looking for a house boy. That is what they say. As Robbie, I agree with their assessment. I feel they are right. Too physically weak for a field hand. Too funny looking and stupid for a house slave.

Any slight hint of self-esteem vanishes from me (as Robbie) in that moment. A buyer takes my mother at a good, fair market price. But leaves me. My mother says nothing as they take her away. She does not even look in my direction. Just walks away. She leaves the way you would leave behind a bag of something useless and no longer needed or wanted. I think as the scene unfolds that maybe she is trying to be kind by making it easy on me. Maybe she does not want me to see the grief on her face. Maybe she is just too beaten and degraded by our lives for anything to matter to her, even her child, and she is genuinely indifferent to leaving her little Robbie behind. But when the sale is made, she simply walks away – no backward glance.

I ache for her. And in that aching, know I am nothing.

The scene changes. And it turns out that Robbie is good for something. He is good for being used sexually at the plantation: first by a black overseer in a tannery where he is sent - then by white men who amuse themselves with him in the fields on hot Georgia afternoons. This bit of attention was the only success Robbie had in this life – he can entertain and amuse and be rewarded with corn liquor and the attention of his captors. In that moment, Robbie feels he has some value.

Maybe Robbie is engaging in an odd way – a scrawny funny faced Negro boy – but his cuteness, of course, fades. And even this small measure of success is taken from him as he ages. The older he gets, the less cute he becomes. He receives less and less and less attention. And then none. Robbie becomes just an old funny looking, toothless black man.

The lesson from Robbie's life? I am not really sure. It may have been one of needing validation from other people for a feeling of self-worth even if that attention is negative. Robbie was a bit of a performer. And I suppose I take after him in that respect. His life, however, was very painful to recall. Robbie, if he did indeed exist and is not really a figment of my imagination, is no doubt buried somewhere in an unmarked grave in the oppressively hot Georgia savannas. A life that seemed to mean nothing and go nowhere.

There is one moment when a slave girl on the plantation shows some interest in Robbie and he allows himself to revisit that image for his entire life: a piece of fresh cornbread she brought from the house wrapped in a scrap of material for him. He cherished the cornbread and more important the memory of the kindness behind the gift. There was a lot of pain in Robbie's life and very little pleasure. Yet when I recall Robbie, it is with fondness: a funny little black boy who did the best he could with what was available to him. And, when you stop to think about, are we not all like that whether we are given a lot to work with at birth or like Robbie, almost nothing at all? We each do the best we can with what we have. Nothing more. Nothing less.

Here is Robbie's story:

ROBBIE
....

I am a little pickaninny
black boy
with a stupid face
Momma tells me I am smart
pay it no mind
maybe that is the problem
ain't got no mind

They bring us to
Market Man
He looks down
Angry face
says
"He's too stupid for the house
too scrawny for the field"

Master he say
"Now wait.
This boy ain't as stupid
as it looks."
Other men laugh

Buyer Man say
"I got enough stupid Africans
at my place
Got no need for anymore
I'll take the bitch gal
but you bring her
picaninny back home"

Mama barely looks at me
maybe she thinks I do be too stupid
too big ears, big mouth
scrawny
That's what Buyer Man says
"scrawny"

Mama barely looks at me
just walks away
maybe she shamed
maybe just do not give it no mind

Now Gregory
He the Master's boy
Whip smart and
natty dresser
likes everyone
everyone likes him
Masters' boy
nothing like me

A Good Boy
A very Good Boy
Best Boy
ain't jealous of him
no Sir
he's a different kind of boy
just better all around

Me? They send me to the tannery
where they got some jobs
for a scrawny stupid looking
little black boy
cleaning out the vats
inside where a grown man
cannot fit
I can and do what I am told

Overseer Fat Man
black man himself
runs me hard
runs me into the ground
runs me onto my knees
says got a special job for me
on my knees
put him in my big
lips and mouth

And suck out his juices
Stay there for a year
in tannery vats
all seasons
winter, summer, harvest

Hot
stinky

But learn my trade
not 'bout cleaning vats
but taking good care of a Man
with my big sassy mouth

Finally, a little less scrawny
I get
sent to the fields

White Men – Master's Kin
break me in
It gets me out of the hot Georgia sun
sometimes a little liquor
corn licker
puts them in a fine mood
to use a little black boy

They take me to the fields
hot as hell
blazes of fires
but Overseer Man knows
what he's been told

Robbie can be a good boy
yessir
special jobs
and smiling all the day

Summer goes to fall
slave gals on the farm
ain't got no use for Robbie
the stupid faced black
white man's boy
But they glad white men use Robbie
not them

One gal Daisy her name
smiles at Robbie
a big smile so wise
and like she knew
Robbie was a smart boy
like his momma said

Gives Robbie a drink of sweet lemonade
in the shade of the house
corn bread another day
...maybe she did...
or maybe just a dream
she takes Robbie in her arms
and lets Robbie make her his queen

Maybe real - maybe just a dream
young Robbie used to get through
special jobs
And Old Robbie'd dream
when no white men say Robbie
is cute and pretty anymore
and stop giving Robbie milk and licker
under the shady tree

Robbie just an old Tom now
toothless - useless
'cept sometimes some man would say that was nice
to use Robbie now he got no teeth

Today Robbie long buried under some shady trees
stupid black boy
no good for nothing
but making men smile
slave to their desires

It took death to
grant emancipation
but finally it did
make little Robbie
now
finally
and forever

FREE.

Chronologically, the next life I will share with you occurs just before (or shortly after) the death of Robbie and the irony couldn't be more obvious. From a victim of racism, my soul chose to come back to this spiritual kindergarten as a victimizer: a completely unapologetically racist.

THE SERGEANT

(INDIA 1800s)

There is only one "time" in the forever time of spirit: NOW.

So, it makes perfect spiritual sense that one moment I am a poor, abused slave boy in Georgia and the next (or just before) I am an arrogant, privileged white supremacist in Her Majesty's service. This is the way past lives work. Today's predator. Tomorrow's prey.

The cosmic logic is as if the golden rule operates in reverse: *expect to have done unto you what you have done onto others*. But timelines in the spirit world are not linear. My sense is that my life as a poor little black boy preceded that of a "sergeant major" in the British Army fighting in India. But they may even have co-existed, and I know some sources believe that souls can split to live incarnated in two bodies at the same time. So, I am inclined to think that karma is independent of time. From the spiritual point of view, there is only NOW.

I know this perspective may sound confusing. I do not claim to understand it logically myself. Let us say you do someone wrong today and as a consequence, you create a karmic debt. Yet it is a debt you may have paid before you were even born. How can that be? Well, if you believe that actions have consequences and accept that time itself is an illusion, it is quite an easy concept to swallow. If all there it is always now, then karmic causal links must be on a whole different plane completely independent of any calendar. Head swirling yet? If you are more than a little confused, it is probably a good sign that you are beginning to get it.

When I first "met" this next life, I was struck by his drill sergeant manner of speaking. He did not really have conversations with anyone. He barked pronouncements. Physically, he was a large, rosy complexioned man, a Yorkshire man born sometime around the start of the nineteenth century or late eighteenth century. Sergeants in the British Army of that time were career soldiers. They were volunteers. Why he chose a life in uniform is obscure to me. Perhaps, finding good work was difficult at home or he may have had a military family background. But whatever drew him to the recruiting table, he found his natural calling in service to the Queen. And his true dedication was to being the boss. He took every advantage of his rank and position to let you know it. He was strict and unforgiving with his men and dismissive of anyone he considered a lesser being. Naturally, this included foreigners, especially those of color.

India in the 19th century was a focus of British colonialism: a jewel in the Crown. The British worked small principalities against one another. The British were better armed and organized and they had a plan: divide, conquer, and rule. My role in this life is to rule a company of men. I say Sergeant Major because that was the way he presented himself to me, but I may have been applying contemporary ideas toward his actual rank. Or, like Private/Corporal Reilly, he may have exaggerated his rank when he introduced himself to me. I do not believe the actual rank of Sergeant Major – other than in the regimental level – was introduced until the early 20th century. But he was definitely the man in charge.

So, let us call him The Sgt. Major just for convenience.

We meet in a desperate battle in a small valley in the Punjab. I am fighting with my pistol and it is not going well. How ironic that, with all the power and glory of the British Empire, there are now just a few of us and so many more of them. There is the confusion and racket of battle, smoke, sounds of bullets ricocheting off rocks or thudding softly into a man's flesh. Screams and curses. I have never been in this kind of battle before. Truth told, I have never really been in any battle. I have been a parade and barracks soldier. A martinet some would say. I discover this day I am not as brave as I always pretended. I look at this discovery as you might look at a scientific hypothesis and say, "oh that is how this works? I never guessed." I am fighting for my life and it is a battle I am destined to lose. At a certain point, I look around. I am shielded behind a rock, but I am out of ammunition and much worse, I am alone. This does not seem possible, and it takes me a moment to realize that this is true. The sun never sets on the British Empire they say, but right now, I am so very alone under the blazing heat of the unforgiving Punjabi sun.

I realize in a terrible awakening that my protection was my rank and bluster. My pretense of manliness came from bullying the men under my charge, men helpless against my blows of words or fists as I am now helpless and utterly alone.

In my Sergeant Major life, I believed I was a superior being. I certainly saw myself as superior to my men. After all, had I not risen from the ranks through hard work, sacrifice, and self-control? Of course I had. The chevrons on my sleeve and my position in the regiment were proof of my accomplishment. My manner and mannerisms were strong and superior. When I am deferential to an officer, it is with a sense of pride. Despite the officer's exalted rank, men like me are the backbone of the British Army. And I would tell you so in the barracks, on the training field, or in the pub as I held court, though I was not a heavy drinker. I would never allow my men to see me out of control. I prided myself that I was never out of control.

Imagine his (and my) surprise to find himself suddenly terrified. With no one to bully, he is on his own and must face his true self. Maybe it is true that all bullies are at heart cowards. This is certainly the case with him.

Charging toward me is the blackest Indian I have ever seen. It is one of those moments when time stands still, and every detail seems highlighted. The attacker looks at me and smiles with a terrible glee. He knows he has his British enemy at his mercy. And he loves it. He revels in it. He smiles at me –

a terrible smile. I see through the Sergeant Major's eyes the rotten teeth that grin at me with the one large gold tooth glistening improbably. Oddly, I focus on that tooth, but just for a moment. Then as if in trance, my glance fixates on a large, curved sword my attacker holds in his hand.

Filled with self-disgust, I find myself on my knees before this man begging to spare my life.

In that moment, I believe for the first time, I see that my life has been built around a false premise. I am not a superior being. I do not have the legendary stiff upper lip under any circumstances. In this moment, I am vulnerable and weak and just a man terrified and begging for his life.

And that is when "I" died.

Funny thing about this death, the Sergeant Major does not go anywhere for a long time. I feel him float over the battle scene. I view with fascination my own corpse. I watch with a curious disinterest as my body is searched for valuables and stripped of anything useful. I never have the experience of my soul moving on and as far as I know, he (part of me perhaps) is still there in the Punjab wondering what happened as he relives his final moments.

My final thought leaving this life was a feeling of deep shame at my cowardice and worst still at being a fraud.

The Sergeant Major: A Man Among

A Queen's Man
through and through
Born in Yorkshire but
The regimental colours
be my brand
Even so always thought I would be buried
one day in sweet Yorkshire land
Not an unmarked grave in a
Godless country's foreign sand

I stand tall and brave
for Queen and Country

I built myself hard
I built myself strong
I built myself like iron
A lion
A Man Among

Spit and polish
Polish and spit
We assemble
On Parade Grounds
our rifles lickety-split
Our buttons gleam
Our minds so keen

My men how they fear me
like they fear God Himself
in the barracks or tramping over sod
in some foreign place we will show
the polliwogs nabobs who is who
and what is what

Black men in black faces
such a disgrace
Animal creatures like beasts
Black faces that slink back into night
In dark retreat
All you see are the whites of their eyes
and shine of grimy teeth

They mumble mumbo-jumbo
Beggars offering blasphemous prayers
to strange idols and unholy Gods
with faces like elephants and

far too many arms
They skulk in crowded alleyways
talking whispered deceit
in their jibby jabby palaver

I look at them as no man
Would dare to look at me
A foot solider confident complete
in the Yorkshire Regiment
victorious in battle
ignorant of defeat

I wake each morning proud to be English
a proud man honor and duty
God, Queen, Country
Englishman brave and true
Not some Lowlife Cockney
Not some arrogant Jew
Or some soulless black faced bugaboo
With treason and murder oozing from its eyes

I know what I know
I know God walks with me
I do not question why
Not until the day I die

And the day I die
seems so long – never ending –
as the traitors ambush us
In a valley – a rocky trap
Set upon by bandits, lying thieves
Who were supposed to be
Our allies and our friends.

And this day I die
seems to last forever
Because time can stand still
in battle
I know this for a fact

In heat, smoke
Crashing of rifles, bullets and tears
No beautiful scarlet laddies in sight
Just me alone
within blackness and smoke
I laugh when I think at least
I kept my powder dry
As I wet myself

Then something crashes into my mind
I see a little boy under a black poplar tree
and a father distant and austere
a man like me
Raising me up to fear
his leather belt snap on my bare backside
A Man Among Himself so he were
Strong and silent scorn
Who I so want to please

A Man Among he was
My Dad
but there are none around me now
And coming near The Bugaboo Punjab Pollywog
My Pollywog
Coming for me saber high
A soulless thing
A big triumphant grin and laughing eyes
Like it's some cosmic joke we are sharing
He and I

But now He is My Lord
and I fall to my knees, cry and beg.
Spare me oh Dark Master and
I will be your slave.
I beg
I cry
I do not know why
And cowardice takes command

Karma the Hindustani dark boys call it
Guilt the Vicar would better understand
Both say you have to pay
But I ask you what crime was mine?

Likely it was simply letting a soulless Pollywog
get the better of an Englishman
whose guard was down
Nothing more
Nothing less

After the noise of battle is gone
I look down on what I had been
Horror. Disgust. Transforming shame.
I spend days in that valley
Maybe am there still now
Vowing next time I will try harder
Next time try harder to be a harder man
not die disgraced
unmarked coward's grave
in some unknown
God forsaken foreign place

At the end of his life, the Master Sergeant was still in denial of the circumstances of his life – that his feelings of superiority and bullying attitude were attempts to cover up feeling of inadequacy perhaps generated by his father's perceived rejection and coldness. He could not or would not face his fear toward its end or his groveling as he begged for mercy from a member of an "inferior race."

It is always nice when an incarnation learns a spiritual lesson and grows dramatically. But that is far from always the case. My soul had to come back again to learn these lessons perhaps starting with the next life I will relate to you.

ERNST

(POLAND 1920s-1945)

In real world chronology, this is the life that most immediately preceded my current incarnation. A *"wannabe"* member of the Master Race.

Like many of the perpetrators of the Holocaust, he was generally non-descript. Like the more notable monsters such as Adolph Eichmann, Ernst's most notable quality was his banality. Evil comes more often in the form of a clerk who victimizes others than it does as a Charles Manson or Adolph Hitler. Evil arrives under the radar in the form of someone who just cannot be bothered facing the true consequences of his or her actions. It is true that some may be genuine sadistic monsters who love their work. But most are simply lazy and pathologically self-centered. And all share the ability to regard other people as categories and objects rather than as flesh and blood humans. Their banality is at core a lack of empathy and perhaps, a deficit of imagination and spiritual development. They have no trouble contributing to the horror millions suffer at their hands. Then, when the workday is done, they go home to their pretty houses and lovely families. They can enjoy a pleasant evening of music, family, and friends after a day of brutality. They are even able to attend religious services in the comfortable assurance that their cruelty is somehow acceptable by God as well as their fellow men. These are true monsters: the banal ones who rob the lives of others and feel justified.

Ernst was one of these.

However, like many of my incarnations, Ernst saw himself as falling short of the standard. Close but no cigar as the saying goes. My spirit seems to be drawn to this type of incarnation. I know it is not alone in doing so. Many people experience self-doubt and feelings of fundamental inferiority. There is even a name for it. Alfred Adler observed this tendency in his patients and coined the term "inferiority complex." So many times in my lives I have felt a sense of isolation and not quite belonging as if everyone else had the manual for successful living. And I did not. When I was little, my mother introduced this idea to me. "Your problem," she said after education from a *Reader's Digest* article on the subject, "is you have an inferiority complex." What she did not know was my soul had been working on this issue for hundreds of years.

My spirit's life as Ernst was one of those incarnations. From my current world-view, Ernst's attitudes and behaviors are reprehensible. Clearly, he was one of those banal, evil men who feel fully justified in their view of the world. Like many of that sort, he was an opportunist, selfish, and not very deep of thought or emotion. He actually would have wanted to be more brutal and callous for the reputation it might bring him. He just did not have the energy or confidence to be a bigger villain.

I came across Ernst while he was in a small satellite concentration camp toward the end of World War II. He was working as an SS auxiliary guard. I do not know much about his earlier life. What I do know is that he was Polish of German ancestry. He looked German, not unlike the way I look today.

Ernst wanted to be like the real SS. But that was not an option for a young Polish man. Perhaps the only reason he got hooked up with the SS was the war's approaching end. The real Germans were desperate for Aryan man-power. And Ernst got his big opportunity. He was young and thrilled to be part of something bigger than himself. But, as a Polish national, there were differences between him and the real SS. His uniform was coarser and less nicely tailored than the true SS. His insignia was slightly different. He was very aware of his inferior status in the break room or barracks socializing with other guards. The German SS stood aloof and apart from the Polish auxiliaries. And

Ernst felt his inferiority acutely. In that way, he was very much like Private Reilly. He aspired to be something he was not and could never be.

I do not think he hated Jews and other prisoners. He was merely indifferent to the suffering inmates. To Ernst, once someone had a number tattooed on their flesh, it is as if they are already dead; they will never leave the camp alive. He knows that this is not the kind of prison where you serve your time and are paroled or released. He knows this is a death camp whether inmates are killed through gas, shooting, starvation, lack of medical attention, exposure, and neglect. He looks at them, starving in their ragged clothes and does not see living human beings. He is looking at corpses that simply have yet to be processed into their final solutions.

Ernst was ambitious to a degree. He knew the Germans were willing to accept virtually anyone who could prove "Aryan" ancestry into the SS and its auxiliaries at this stage of the war. Ernst took advantage of this knowing though that he would never be the kind of elite Aryan that the SS portrayed in its posters. He was a *wannabe*. Ernst understood and accepted this unlike Private Reilly who had hopes of advancement. Ernst felt unworthy. But he was happy to get the pay and prestige that came from being part of something he respected. His main complaint was he did not like his uniform. He thought it was too coarse and not as nicely tailored as "the real thing."

Much of his life in those final days is spent patrolling the perimeter and feeling somewhat important. He proudly shoulders a rifle he never shot in anger, reveling in its power. And this is how Ernst died: on a boring, routine patrol around the camp perimeter. It was toward the very end of the war in Poland. Many of the regular SS had mysteriously been "reassigned." Ernst was walking his assigned route aware something was amiss but not fully comprehending the gravity of the situation.

When the Russian infantry come into view, Ernst is strangely calm. He is struck by an odd thought. He finds himself at a moment of mortal danger comparing his uniform's quality to the crude Soviet garb. He feels an unexpected moment of pleasure as he judges his uniform as superior. The Russians look to him like ragamuffins. Ernst feels he looks like the real thing: a true SS Master Race

Man. While savoring this thought, he is shot through the chest, never having a chance to fire his own weapon. Ernst falls on the muddy ground feeling his uniform become moist. His last thoughts flicker to his childhood playing in the fields with his brothers – happy and innocent. Unlike Private Reilly's sudden death, there is no sense of leaving consciousness with a bang. Ernst simply hovers for a moment over the scene, watching his body in the crumpled, bloody uniform shocked by the suddenness of it all and the finality. Gradually, the scene fades. His spirit moves upward, leaving the sordid scene behind.

You might ask what was such a seemingly meaningless banal life about? What, if anything, did my spirit learn from this sad experience? Perhaps it was the idea of being unwilling to settle for such a petty and unenlightened existence. Ernst was willing to participate in the dehumanization of others for a little security and prestige. Another lesson from Ernst is how easy it can be to classify a group of people as less than human – a perspective I carry with me strongly in this life.

But my major takeaway from this life is a strong desire to be the real thing and the awareness of the need for self-acceptance. I think at the end of this life, Ernst did feel like the real thing – pathetic as that may sound – yet realized in the end it meant nothing. He had sold himself very short.

Karmically, I came into this life with a need to make amends to people who are dehumanized. I became the child of someone who looked down on others and claimed to admire Hitler. My early years were spent as a victim of his assault on my self-esteem and dignity. My challenge was to create my own value. And I am happy to say that I am succeeding though not without some bumps and bruises along the way.

My mission in this incarnation is now to help others see their own value and break through self-imposed limiting beliefs.

ALMOST A MASTER RACE

I got in toward the end
it was almost over
when I begin
but I need
to be one of
them

Uniform of the SS
black and proud
a dagger
pointed at
enemies of the Reich

Even though I am only
a Pole
I am proud to be
almost pure Aryan stock
chosen
to be among my own kind
A Master
making Europe safe
and free
under the Führer
fighting for civilization
and racial purity

The ones behind the wire
with the numbers on their arms
already dead
I know
they know it too
their crime being born
A Gypsy, Communist
or Jew

I do not have to think about them
they have been processed
cataloged, numbered
and condemned
What bothers me is
the talk in
our common room
where true Germans
stand apart
and look down on me
They have no right
my blood pure as theirs
but still they see me
as a Pole
little more than a Christian Jew
so I prove to them
I am a strong and Aryan Man
and fierce as any of them
I strut
sing the Horst Wessel song
so strong
but sometimes my uniform's
coarseness and poor tailoring
remind me
I am not really one of them

I came in toward the end
it is almost over when I begin
everything is scarce
corners cut
My boots feel cheap
though I polish shine them
until I can see
the reflection of an Aryan man
looking back

And now things are changing
Some of the others have disappeared
the wire section I patrol
gets bigger
every week
I feel the emptiness
something bad about to happen
the prisoners sense it too
instead of waiting for death
some waiting
for something else
and whisper I know
Liberation
by the Russians
the Commies
Jews to liberate Jews

Then one day
Only us Poles left now
the Commandant Himself disappears
telling us in perfect high German
"reinforcements will be coming soon"
From where?
When?
How?
Not even proper toilet tissue
in the latrines

I got into this late
so late
almost over when I begin
but I need
to be
one of the Big Men
and I am
until the end

an SS MAN
holding the rifle
my words absolute sway
among the already dead
with numbers tattooed
A master of the master race
How they dread me
the almost dead
as I walk and talk
a proud – SS MASTER MAN

I do not hear when Russians
come into view
just feel a rumbling
a chill in the air
then the slam
into my chest
twirling me around
so that as I fall
last thoughts wondering
from where it came
not a rumbling tank that killed me
just a sniper man
and why me?

My uniform so superior
to the crude Russian man
I glimpse as I fall
in such a lonely place
how sad
for this to be my fate
a Master Race MAN
lying in
dust
just outside
my prison camp's
mocking unlocked gates

The next life experience I will share with you was a victim of her times and gender. And this is the way it seems to go in the cycle of reincarnations. One day we are a victim, the next an auxiliary SS Guard in a death camp. Hopefully, though, another piece in the great cosmic puzzle falls into place with each incarnation until we finally graduate to whatever it is that follows this dance of life after life.

LENA

(RURAL RUSSIA – CZARIST TIMES – DATE UNKNOWN)

I felt like I was the luckiest girl in the world.

To have a husband who not only did not beat me, but also had a trade and seemed to like me was an unheard-of bounty for a young woman like me in my village.

One way to organize your past life journey is simply to ask yourself (or your spirit) what prior life (if any) wished to be explored for your development and for that experience to come forward. This is certainly a legitimate approach. The assumption is that the soul knows what it needs. I often use it with clients to great effect. Another way to structure a past life journey is to go back into past lives in order to bring forth a skill or quality that you wish to incorporate your current life. A third is to directly explore an issue or relationship from the perspective of a past life's impact on a current incarnation. So, when I had a chance to volunteer at a past life therapist training, I asked to explore my relationship with my wife in our prior lives. A couple of other people in the class also looked to their relationships. Their stories are not mine to tell. But I will share with you that each of them found profound insights. And I will tell you about one of my clients who has given me permission to share this next little story.

She was a woman who had a pattern of becoming romantically involved with men who eventually end up betraying her. I know many women, as well as some men, who read this will think this is not that unusual. The statistics on long-term faithfulness can be daunting. Half of all marriages end in divorce often with unfaithfulness being a factor. Though many men can be trusted to be monogamous and faithful, some cannot. She would become involved with one of these and inevitably she would catch him in a lie and end the relationship.

I am sure you know of – and perhaps even know personally – people like my client who obsess about whether their partner is cheating on them. Maybe they stalk them on social media, check their cell-phone records, or drive by at night to see if there are strange cars. Perhaps they go so far as to hire a private detective. This was not that kind of the situation in my client's case. She would catch him in a lie accidentally and be genuinely surprised. She would "discover" that the man she thought belonged to her had been in a relationship for months, maybe even years, with another woman. It would come as a great sadness to her, an overwhelming shock that would send her to isolate herself in her room for days. Eventually, she would straighten herself out and soon find another to repeat the cycle. This pattern of being blindsided was destroying her peace of mind.

What brought her to hypnosis for past life regression was an unusual situation. She had become involved with a new man. She found him incredibly interesting and exciting and had the idea that "this was THE ONE." But surprisingly, this man said to her in no uncertain terms, "I want you to know I don't do monogamy. I do not believe in it. I really like being with you, but I don't do exclusive relationships." In response to this startling declaration, she heard her own mind thinking, "I can fix him." She was not an unintelligent woman. She recognized that this thinking was anything but rational. It is one thing to be blindsided by a man who sneaks behind your back. It is quite another when he tells you that is exactly what he intends to do and makes no apology for *and then you go forward thinking you can fix it*. There are soulmates in life and if we are lucky, we get to spend a lifetime with them. But there are also "soul dates." This was obviously another one of those for her if she was willing to play by his rules.

She had been through years of therapy to address this issue without success. So, all else having failed, she thought that perhaps there was a past life pattern involved. Please understand that every time a person gets stuck in therapy, a past life issue is not necessarily the cause. Ordinarily, looking in one's current life through psychotherapy, you will find the root cause eventually. But you must be patient, and your success may depend on whether you have the right therapist for you. Just because you hate your boss does not mean he was your arch enemy in 18th century France or your torturer in ancient Persia. Sometimes he is just a jerk, or he reminds you of your big brother who used to tease you and lock you in a closet when you were little. But sometimes you may find yourself thinking I have done this before – that this seems familiar and somehow bigger than me and nothing I have done seems to help break this pattern. This was her case.

So, we did the hypnotic induction and past life regression protocols and she found herself living as a concubine for a minor prince somewhere in the Mideast. This was a culture where the position of concubine was a perfectly honorable role. The problem was that she and the prince had an unusually intense relationship: not what was expected or typical between a lord and a concubine. What is more he had said to her – or implied – that he would promote her to be a wife. He implied not only would she be a wife but the most important wife. Somehow, word of this got back to the ears of the real head wife and my client found herself imprisoned in a dark and dank place.

I am not sure how long she stayed there. But eventually she died there through a combination of poor nutrition, cold and – you might say – of a broken heart. All the while she was imprisoned, she was literally waiting for her prince to come and rescue her. She died alone and bewildered.

As I have said often here, my sense is that each life ends with some issue that is unresolved and some that are resolved. When we investigate past lives, it is often the lives when there is some large unresolved question that we drop into most easily. Her questions entombed before her lonely departure from this Earth were, "When will he come to save me? What could I have done differently to make him love me?" She had brought this longing for completion – for salvation – for romantic fulfillment – into her current life. Over and over again, she would enter a new relationship with hope only to be disappointed and dashed into despair.

So, you might be wondering, what happened next? Well, this story is about real life and in this real life what happened was she went forward. She ended up dating that man. She liked him. She wanted to be in relationship with him. But she became involved literally without expectations and felt incredible freedom and peace of mind. I do not know whether they lived happily ever after. That is not the point. My client went on to live happily I am sure with or without a prince to rescue her from her self-imposed tomb.

But back to my story.

As I entered the hypnosis trance with the intention of seeing whether my wife and I had been connected in a prior life, I quickly got a vivid impression of a blacksmith. He was strong with big muscles and a black beard. His black-smith shop was a shed in a small village. I sensed this was Russia. The lane in front of the shop was muddy and the shop was open to it. There was the clanging of mallets on metal. Smoke from the fire singed my eyes and the smell was familiar and distinctive. I felt such a sense of gratitude for this man and my situation. This was my husband. I almost started laughing out loud when I realized that I am experiencing my wife Maria as a blacksmith in rural Russia during czarist times. And I feel like the luckiest person in the world. This is how I met Lena.

I was bringing my husband's dinner. And I was filled with gratitude at how well my life had turned out. The facilitator asked me what my "husband" said when I brought him his dinner. I literally laughed out loud. I told the class "nothing – he is a man of few words." It seemed this was just a nice, happy, and uneventful life. But as I have remarked before, no one gets out of life unscathed. In this spiritual kindergarten, there is a curriculum and even examinations along the way. The facilitator asks whether there was anything unresolved from this life and I feel an incredible sense of sadness and deep loss. I realized that there was a significant tragedy in this otherwise pleasant life. One day, the Cossacks or the czarist military came into our village and simply took all the men for mandatory military service, including my husband. And once this happened in our village, the women mourned because we knew we would likely never see our men again. This would have been bad enough, I suppose. But I soon came to see that a few days before this I had heard a warning from the other women of the village that this was about to happen. I had heard rumors that they were coming to take the men. And I had tried to convince my husband (my current wife in this life) that we had to flee. I had begged and pleaded. I had said we must pack up and leave. I said we could come back later. But I begged him to leave while we could. And I could not convince him. After all, who was I? I was only a woman. Even though my husband was kind and loved me, he did not listen.

After he was taken, I missed him every single day and I never once lost that feeling of gratitude for having had such a wonderful marriage and wonderful man. My life was hard for many years. I worked in fields and did odd jobs. We had three children before he left: two boys and a girl. I recall the end of this life clearly. It is in my little hut and I have been ill for quite some time.

I am frail with white hair and as I pass into whatever it is that is next, my daughter holds my hand. There is love here. Much love. But there is also an unresolved issue as I leave this life. The tragedy – that became the central theme of this life. My one regret was that I was not able to convince my husband to listen to me. I knew we should go. We should flee. I felt it in every fiber of my being. I knew I was right. And circumstances prove me correct. But I could not even get his attention. I die with this horrible regret heavy on my mind and heart.

I left that life as Lena with a strong mission: that mission is to be heard. And all my life I have been a communicator. College instructor. Advertising copywriter and creative director. And now hypnotist, coach and past life facilitator. I talk a lot. I listen a lot, too. And now there is this little book which is my way of telling my stories to the best of my ability without restraint – to be known, heard, and seen.

I think Lena would be pleased.

Lena's Story: The Magpie's Lament

I was the luckiest girl in my village
Others knew it too
Some jealous
Some glad for me

Wife of Viktor
blacksmith strong and true
man of substance
no man's fool

Me? Young and foolish
Only a girl
Knowing nothing at all
But what mother whispered
on my wedding day

And despite mother's warnings
my husband did not beat me
not even once
this may seem a small thing to you
but to me
it is everything
a man like that - kind and strong
a man like that – brave and true

A man of few words
his actions say it all
that I belong to him

and safe within
his strong embrace

I keep our home
best I can
let him take pleasure with me
gladly
Cook
Clean
I do all with joy

The luckiest girl in the village
with such a strong, good, silent man
not some clumsy
cruel
farmer boy

I love to watch him
sweating
as he hammers iron
in his blacksmithing shed
making tools
fitting horses' shoes
his thick black beard
so manly

He is known as a good man
hard-working
honorable
and mine

And so we live peacefully
as anyone ever did
I love to cook his favorite meals
and make his clothes

I bear his children
two boys and a girl
I give them to him
my gifts

I am just a woman
This I know
As good as I can be
And Viktor is a good man
a wonderfully good man
but he is a man and men
do not see
what a woman knows
to be true

The women in the village
say Cossacks will come in the spring
and take the men
to fight some foreign war
in distant lands

It has happened before
the old ones say
and men do not come back
when they go away

I know they know this
to be true
these wise old widows
dressed in black
and though winter
is behind us
I feel a rising chill.

I feel it in my heart
and the little hairs
on back of my neck

I know they are right
a woman knows

I tell Viktor we must run
before this terrible thing
takes our peaceful life

My little garden where I grow vegetables
the goat we keep
the chickens

Our children at their chores
The night before the fire
the warmth of my husband
and my baby at my side

Our precious little life

But Viktor is a man
and does not listen
to a woman like me
he says you are being silly
listening to old women's tales
you should be wiser Lena
you should not be so frail

My husband is kind
with a loving smile
but he is a man
he cannot see what I feel
he cannot know what I know

He does not wake in the night
dreaming Cossack horses' hooves
breaking the village's peace
But I do

I plead
I beg
until he says stop
and I know he will hear no more

Then one day they come
Sunday when the village is
at church

The priest tries to stop them
they strike him down

They come and take my Viktor
I fall to the ground
and cry
my children
clinging to me and I to them

Another weak broken woman
I watch them take the men
never to return
and become a widow that day
a widow whose husband still lives
but far far away

A widow with children
to clothe and feed
I work every day
to keep my babies alive
It is hard
it hurts

But to my dying day
I tell anyone who wants to listen
that I was the luckiest girl in my village
A man so strong and kind

A man who did not beat me
Who knew how to make iron
bend to his will
A man I was so proud to call mine.

My husband is a silent man.
I speak often - a lot - for a blacksmith's wife
I always thought I had so much to say
And he lets me chatter off and away
but I do not think he ever
really listens or so I came to believe

He says I am like a magpie
his Lena the magpie
always chat chattering
But I know he likes the sound of my voice
as I clean and cook
and make and mend his clothes

And now there is nothing more to say

I hope you have benefited from listening to my stories. I also hope you become motivated to do your own past explorations.

As I said at the outset, there is no way to know whether all these lives really happened. Were they really drawn from my Soul's memory or some universal database? Or did they simply spring from my subconscious mind?

Personally, I would say it really does not matter because I have benefited from each one. Hopefully, you will from your explorations if you join me on this path.

But past life exploration to me is like a game of **three-dimensional chess in your search for peace, personal power and spiritual growth**. You are not only focused on this life but all the connecting ones.

The perspectives you gain and results you achieve can be amazing.

The next life I will share with you is the one with which I am most familiar: my soul's current incarnation.

JOHN KOENIG

(UNITED STATES – 1948 – THE PRESENT)

As I said when we started, I doubt the story of my life would have kept your attention this long. I have not been famous or even notorious. Like the great mass of humanity, I have essentially been a peasant – a modern peasant living by far the most comfortable of any of my incarnations. I have also been blessed not to live during times of great social or climatic upheaval. I have been privileged as a 20th/21st Century American to live with an abundance, comfort, and security that far exceeds anything that 99.9% of history's humanity could have hoped for.

Any problems I have faced have been, to a degree, of my own making. It has always been my response to events rather than the events themselves that has caused me suffering.

But I cannot be much clearer than that about what my life is really about. My past life journeying has told me that each life usually embodies one simple theme. These may seem obvious to others, but rarely are they clear to us as we live a life. That is what people mean when they say that when you die your past streams before you. Each life does end with at least one question left unresolved for further exploration. Since I am still in this life, much for me is still an open question. Maybe you can guess at it from the stories I have shared with you but it is not that clear to me.

So let me start to end this little book by going back to the beginning: my beginning. I have heard it said – Louise Hay and many others – that we choose our parents. We cast our parents and family as the perfect players to work out whatever issue we need to resolve. And we choose everything else about ourselves: our genetics, finances, social status, gender, and the larger political and cultural landscape into which we find ourselves. If our lives are dramas, these elements are the set designs and the master plot in which our characters develop.

My story?

I chose to be born in Harlem late one night. It was at the Flower Fifth Avenue Hospital. I was a child of German-Irish-English-Scots lineage. I started my life experience as the only northern European Caucasian child in the nursery filled with souls who have chosen to be incarnated as beautiful little black boys and girls. I was easy to pick out. I was the pinkish one likely crying his head off. I wonder if Robbie – my black slave boy incarnation – had anything to do with that.

The parents I chose were a 19-year-old woman – little more than a girl herself – from Northern Georgia and a 21-year-old union laborer from the lower east side of Manhattan. People come together in different ways. There is some magic that brings people of the most unlikely combinations together. My father had been in the Army and was stationed near Washington, D.C. at the time. My mother's father had died when my mother was barely two years old. So, she grew up also without a father. These were depression years. Naturally, there was very little money to clothe, feed, and educate a half-orphan child. My mother was still in high school when she and my dad met. Like my father, my mother was intelligent. She enjoyed her literature studies especially and was the favorite of some of her teachers. They offered support for her to go on to college, an unusual step for a woman in the 1940s.

My father was young and handsome. A working class, fast-talking New Yorker. His own father had died suddenly when my father was twelve. I have often thought their half-orphan status was part of what kept them together through the ups and downs. My dad was one of those men who felt he "could've been a contender" had not circumstances conspired against him. One of these may have been his marriage to my mother itself.

My father had many good qualities and some less admirable ones. His lack of education gave him a chip on his shoulder that he carried his entire life. My father never trusted people (especially men) who had education, power, or privilege. He was disrespectful and resentful. My dad was what you might call a rebel without much of a cause. Oh, there were moments of triumph in his life. And, as I mentioned, my father had a commitment to family perhaps because, like my mom, he grew up with only one parent and clung to the family they built together. He was hardworking and had an eye for making money. My father also has what is politely called a drinking problem. Eventually, he caught himself on and spent the last forty-five years of his life in sobriety. But my father had much in common with my past lives as Private Reilly and Ernst. Both also felt that life circumstances had cheated them out of their rightful place in the world.

However, there was a consequence to my choice of my father as my father. When a child is raised by an active alcoholic he or she never knows what to expect. Their survival is dependent on an autocrat whose mood will vary depending on the amount of alcohol consumed. Both the Egyptian cattle rancher and Brother Thomas would have understood the deeply ingrained mistrust of authority such an upbringing creates. It is no accident that I have self-employed for over thirty-five years.

I am sure my convicted murderer who discovered a bladder full of fortified wine was a great way to beat the hangman or the stone age hunter who vowed never to experience that kind of pain again would have been part of the selection committee that settled on my father to be the man who would stimulate me to generate my own sense of worth and value.

My father's father was German-American. He died in 1939. At the time of his death, Adolf Hitler had recently been celebrated on the cover of *Time* magazine as the man of the year. Many German-Americans had great pride in the new Germany. My grandfather – my father's father – was one of these. Every Sunday, the family would assemble in front of the radio and listen to

German marching songs. It was still acceptable for a young lower eastside New Yorker to take pride in the ideal of a new Germany arising from the ashes of the Versailles Treaty.

My grandfather died with a sudden heart attack. He left my father, his older sister, and their mom to fend for themselves. My dad left school as soon as he was able and began to work as a truck driver's helper to support his mother and sister. My father was 12 years old. I believe he admired his own father whom he called Pop. Naturally, he also grew up admiring the new Germany his father so admired.

Due to the chip on his shoulder no doubt, my father liked to tease people, especially the Irish, Jewish, and Italians. He created a persona of a right wing "Nazi" to torment his Jewish friends and associates. He referred to Italians as Wops and to Irish as "donkeys" – derogatory even though he himself was 50% Irish ancestry. I do not believe my father was prejudiced in the way many from his era and social status were. My father just loved to get a rise out of people. I think it made him feel superior and, perhaps, helped him to counter his own feelings of inadequacy. My British Sergeant Major would have understood.

But out of his element (the Lower Eastside New York Bowery Boy world), my father did not feel very comfortable. I remember watching with surprise at the way he would defer to people in authority – especially men with suits and ties. My strong, commanding, bigger-than-life father could be visibly intimidated by white-collar people. He found well-spoken men with good vocabularies especially intimidating. And this was, with a bit of cosmic irony, exactly the kind of man I would grow up to be.

But I believe my father was genuinely a good man at core who did his best. He cared about his family and would go any lengths to protect his own. As I grew into maturity, I came to see the ways he showed his family commitment, not in words but in actions. I think most of us have trouble picturing our parents as young and in love. Many marriages, even the best, can seem improbable. Each is a karmic contract as unique as a fingerprint or snowflake – no two absolutely alike. As half orphans, I believe my parents struck a deal to ally themselves against the world. Their mission became to build and maintain a family, creating a stability neither had known as children. But there was an adjustment time, and I came along when they were just learning how to be together.

This is the cast of characters I chose for leading roles in my life this time around. And I honor them as individuals and souls who overcame much adversity to build a life together. I say this without reservation, despite the times when they fell short of my ideals of parenthood. I believe, by the way, that it is a spiritual axiom that no one becomes a true adult until he or she accepts his parents exactly as they were and not as they would like them to have been and forgives them for any shortcomings whether real or simply imagined. Although our stories are intertwined, however, this is not my father or mother's autobiography. This is my soul's story. What is relevant to that story is the impact their souls had on mine in this incarnation. My father's own feelings of inadequacy led him to put people down to raise his own feelings of self-importance. My dad was a jokester and experienced pleasure from belittling others. He often couched his hostility behind humor which let him get away with things he might otherwise have not. But people got his message, especially his children. His judgements could be devasting and were all encompassing. He rarely was content to criticize a behavior, his target was a person's sense of self-worth. One of his favorite put-downs was to refer to someone as a phony. Another was to say a certain person was "nothing." By the world's standards my father did not accomplish much until his mid-40s. He was a semi-professional boxer early in his life. He would have loved to be a great athlete but either did not have the talent or dedication. I doubt my father was fully aware of his many good qualities. Objectively, he was handsome and charismatic, a natural leader. But his resentment and mistrust of anyone who achieved success in the world always held him back. In my father's mind, most people who succeeded were frauds who came by their success through dishonesty, luck or privilege. For example, my father said that Beatles John Lennon, Paul McCartney and

Ringo Starr were nothing. George Harrison was the one with "all the talent" my father would say. He couldn't conceive of the possibility that all were talented men who worked together in a successful collaboration.

To protect myself from my dad's disdain, I learned to conceal what I truly felt at home as well as in the world. I even adopted a strategy of presenting myself as the opposite of what I truly felt as protection to cover my true feelings. The rapist in the southwest United States would understand this habit.

Also, my father was a great karmic pick for someone who had been until recently a Polish SS Guard in a prior incarnation. My father presented himself on occasion as a Nazi *wannabe*, but it wasn't, I believe, his reality. It was just a pose designed to elicit a reaction. I am sure my dad's rational self knew better. Never less, I became the victim of cruelty and a degree of dehumanization by a man who was but a parody of Nazi ideology.

On the other hand, my mother was a chronic worrier. And she came by her worry habit very understandably. Her life was difficult as a child. Financial lack, split families, and the experience of being a fatherless child during the Depression gave her a negative attitude toward life. Like my dad, she made the family her most important frame of reference. She could be fierce in her defense of her sons: myself and my three brothers. It was a family joke that she never liked any of the women her sons became involved with. My youngest brother was for many years a bachelor; however, he had a female dog that he cared deeply about. My father jokingly said once that the only female that my mother liked was my youngest brother's dog Jingles. My mother had a dry sense of humor and responded in a droll way "I'm not too sure about Jingles."

I inherited my mother's tendency to worry and combined that with my father's mistrust of authority. When I look back in writing this brief narrative, I see I have felt betrayed by those who were in charge time after time. Betrayed by the pharaoh's men who took me as a slave. Betrayed when I was a palace guard by a royal family when I was demoted to end my days as a field hand. Betrayed by an entire social system as a black boy slave in antebellum Georgia.

You remember that I began this narrative with imagining my own death. In that experience, I met my father and mother in a remarkable way. All was forgiven. All was transformed. Words are inadequate to explain the feeling of deep love as the three of us went on toward the light. I sensed in that moment that human life is like a theatrical performance. We adopt personas. We get to wear costumes. There are plot twists as our lives interact with larger events. Sometimes there are blessings in the form of *deus ex machina* like being struck sober by what seems like a divine intervention.

I have heard it said that the day we die is like any other day only shorter. My experience as a past-life voyager confirms this. Real life is not at all like fiction. In fiction, the issues a person faces get resolved and then a person passes into death. Reality is quite different. Life just ends. We simply exit in the middle of our drama. It may be on a battlefield, alone in a desert, hung on a noose or in our bed surrounded by loved ones. But a life just ends. Poof. Inevitably, loose ends and unresolved issues surround us as silent observers of our demise. For this reason, I believe living each day as if it may be your last is perhaps the highest form of human enlightenment. But when the drama that is our life is over what do we then become?

This is a central question that I believe everyone must answer for him or herself. My father and mother both believed that when you die that is the end – that there is nothing, no hereafter, only here and now. I doubt that they gave much thought to the issue. I, on the other hand, have given a lot thought to this kind of thing. Maybe that is the African shaman in me mixed with the theological scholar Brother Thomas. As a young man, I took to heart the admonition by Plato that "the unexamined life is not worth living." The questions of what life is – what it is to be human – what consciousness is have been on my mind for many years.

Long before I started this journey of past life exploration, I had the idea that humanity is in the process of evolution. I have come to believe that each soul, yours and mine included, is evolving and moving toward unity and unification with That Which Creates This. You can call it God. I usually do. Why not? You can call it whatever you wish. The best we – or any religion can do – is get an approximate idea of its true nature. There was a time when my perspective on the very idea of God was corrupted by the fantasies and hypocrisies of the religion I was born into. I have learned to separate my relationship with this creator from any religious structure. I think both my African shaman and even Brother Thomas would be proud of me.

I am grateful to be able to access the energies of each of these incarnations to help me cope with the challenges of this life. When needed I am able to access the ambition of Private Reilly or Ernst, The SS *wannabe,* the wonder and curiosity of my Shaman and his inquiring nature, the ability to entertain as a coping strategy of Robbie the slave boy, Una's coaching skills, Lena's love, gratitude and abiding loyalty, my Guard to the Pharoah's royal family's capacity for selfless worship, my prehistoric hunters' ability to function as part of a team, my medieval murderer and Sergeant Major's masculinity, Zeke the rapist's resourcefulness and ability to function independently and Brother Thomas' scholarly attitude and spirituality. In meditation, I work with these entities to help them find peace. I believe this practice has made me more of an integrated whole as I include their evolutions as part of my current incarnation. And, yes, my past life journeying is far from over as I grow and more of my past life experiences call for discovery.

This notion of evolution is important to me as part of my path. In my life journey, I have been blessed to run into teachers and organizations that provided direction as to what is next and all have pointed to the possibility of progress and spiritual growth. I have, in fact, dedicated myself to the possibility of human growth through adversity. I put a name on this new species we are becoming: HomoDeus, a new kind of human. I see this new way of being as approaching a more perfect union with God – co-creators if you will. And, to me, this is not the work of a single lifetime and I strive to bring all of mine into the task. This is the work of many lifetimes. It is the mission of many souls reaching together toward our shared destiny.

I believe also there are soul families. Perhaps you and I share the same one. It is possible that you were guided to acquire this book because you and I have known each other before as part of the same spiritual master group. I believe there are such things as soul mates and believe that I have been blessed to find and be found by mine – a wonderful soul that I love with all my heart. In a dance with each other, she and I have both grown. We have been each other's teachers, friends, and lovers.

I am not going to bore you with my own conclusions and speculations about theology. I will not even touch what happens between lives in detail. There are many other authors who do this very well. I will say that I have felt what it is like to be part of a Soul Family basking in a shared bliss. My own experience guided by a gifted facilitator gave me a glimpse of this time of reflection and communication. It convinced me that there is nothing to fear in death. It just does not always seem that way here in spiritual kindergarten where fear is as ubiquitous as the air we breathe.

Nor will I speculate as to why my children chose me to be their father. I only hope the lessons they learned from me were not passed on in such a heavy-handed way as those I learned from my own father. But it seems impossible not to pass down some of our defects and challenges to our children no matter how hard we try. I believe most parents, if they are honest, will agree. Though perhaps you will find some comfort in the thought that your children chose you (or will choose you). It is never much consolation to tell yourself, "karma made me do it." We are still responsible for our own choices and actions. But I do believe we all do our best one life at a time. And I believe there is comfort in the hope that we get the chance to clean up this life's missteps in our next incarnation in this spiritual kindergarten known as planet Earth.

My mission in this life?

I think my mission is to take advantage of relatively easy circumstances in this incarnation to grow as a person and an evolving soul. I believe my mission here is also to help others — perhaps you — on their journeys to wholeness and unity. I have no doubt that I will be asked back to this spiritual kindergarten for more than a few more lives until I get it right. Maybe you and I have already met in our past life journeys or will meet again in those of our futures. In the meantime, my Soul thanks Yours for sharing this journey with me and I wish you growth and peace if, inspired by this little book, you choose to explore your autobiographies.

Our Autobiographies: Yours and Mine

If all the world is a stage,
you and I the cast,
who watches the show?

God? Our Higher Selves?
Our Souls?

or are these dramas
simply stored on
forgotten shelves
forever unread
forever unseen?

Perhaps not even
by ourselves
unless old age finds us musing
"Yes. This was me.
I lived.
An amazing dream
now coming to
an end."

Is that all there is?
Tales told
by myself
to myself?
For no one?
Nothing?

*Empty and meaningless
Like a play performed
In a theater where all
the seats are empty?*

*Did it happen at all?
Not even a dream?
Just a nothing
for no one.*

*Or do you and I
play a role
in this Great Epic
with a Divine Audience
in rapt attention to every
twist and turn of our plots?
A series of
never-ending beginnings.
Each a step
closer to transcendence
to the Divine?
Something at stake
of far more significance
than any life's success,
failure, sadness, grief
or joy*

*So, I choose to believe
And invite you dear reader
To join me.
Join me
in this Magical quest*

*To be
not your mind
or your body*

but a Soul witnessing
Divinity Growing
Infinite Unfolding

Becoming one with Whatever
Creates This Universe
The Cosmic Observer
Universal Creator
Master Storyteller
That Which Creates This
Before the Beginning
Past the End
Always present
Waiting to be found
and then re-found
Over and over
joyously
rediscovering and
rediscovered within